Stories from the Front of the Room

Stories from the Front of the Room

How Higher Education Faculty of Color Overcome Challenges and Thrive in the Academy

Michelle Harris, Sherrill L. Sellers, Orly Clerge, and Frederick W. Gooding Jr.

ROWMAN & LITTLEFIELD
Lanham • Boulder • New York • London

Published by Rowman & Littlefield
A wholly owned subsidiary of The Rowman & Littlefield Publishing Group, Inc.
4501 Forbes Boulevard, Suite 200, Lanham, Maryland 20706
www.rowman.com

Unit A, Whitacre Mews, 26-34 Stannary Street, London SE11 4AB

British Library Cataloguing in Publication Information Available

Library of Congress Cataloging-in-Publication Data Available

ISBN 978-1-4758-2516-9 (cloth : alk. paper)
ISBN 978-1-4758-2517-6 (pbk. : alk. paper)
ISBN 978-1-4758-2518-3 (electronic)
∞™ The paper used in this publication meets the minimum requirements of American National Standard for Information Sciences Permanence of Paper for Printed Library Materials, ANSI/NISO Z39.48-1992.

Printed in the United States of America

Contents

Acknowledgments vii

Introduction 1

I: Colleagues **11**

1 Highlights of Research Literature on Colleagues and Faculty of
Color: Can't Get No Respect 13

2 Letters 17

3 Mentor Essay: Standing Firm Upon Unsteady Ground 37
Alford Young Jr., University of Michigan

II: Students **41**

4 Research Exploring Bias in Student Ratings of Teachers 43

5 Letters 49

6 Mentor Essay: Don't Forget to Reflect On and Fight Your Own
Biases 63
Mary Pattillo, Northwestern University

III: Tenure **67**

7 Literature on Teaching, Research, and Service 69

8 Letters 75

9 Mentor Essay: Tenure 89
Juan Battle, City University of New York (CUNY)

IV: Administration 95

10 Literature on Administrative Contexts with Focus on
Recruitment and Retention 97

11 Letters 103

12 Mentor Essay: Reflections on Higher Ed Administration 119
Harvey Charles, University of Albany

V: Climate 127

13 Major Themes in the Research on Faculty of Color and Campus
Climate 129

14 Letters 133

15 Mentor Essay: The Talk 147
Eduardo Bonilla-Silva, Duke University

Afterword: The Historical Moment 151

Index 155

About the Editors 157

About the Contributors 159

Acknowledgments

We first want to thank the various authors herein for sharing their stories. We also appreciate the indispensable peer reviews from Sharon F. Gooding, Rodney D. Coates, and Gretchen McAllister. This is a much better book thanks to your feedback. The Office for the Advancement of Research at Miami University also provided support for the volume.

Introduction

Dear Reader,

Diversifying the professoriate has been a long-term project for many research universities and liberal arts colleges across the country. Higher education institutions have recruited an increasing number of faculty of color and built more racially inclusive administrations, programs, and departments. Faculty of color bring value orientations and philosophies to the university that are unique and productive to higher education (Antonio, 2002). They broaden the scope of scholarship in vital ways. However, despite some advances in recruitment, studies demonstrate that faculty of color in predominantly white institutions experience higher levels of discrimination, cultural taxation, and emotional labor than their white colleagues (Joseph and Hirshfield, 2011; Stanley, 2006; Turner, González, and Wood, 2008), all of which undermines their scholarship, pedagogy, and social experiences.

Stories from the Front of the Room includes a diverse array of narratives about how faculty of color navigate through their everyday experiences on campus. Our intent is to present a more complete picture of life in the academy—one that documents how faculty of color are tested by its structures, but also how they can survive and thrive within their respective educational institutions.

Contributing authors were asked to paint a picture of an event or a series of events in a nontraditional format—a letter. The letter format of the volume allows the reader to gain a richer understanding of the day-to-day meetings, interactions, e-mails, and emotions that nudge faculty of color toward marginal positions in the ivory tower and, in many cases, how they break through these barriers.

Providing examples of a wide variety of experiences from different instructors of different genders and races across different institutions and disci-

1

plines from various regions of the country, the letters are addressed to colleagues, students, administrators, mentors, and friends. Some speak of invisibility, discrimination, or exclusion in relation to the writers' race, ethnicity, religion, class, citizenship status, and gender. Others are expressions of love and thanks for mentors, family, friends, and allies. The epistolary style allowed contributors to more freely express themselves, without having to cleave to the traditional rules of academic writing and citation. The powerful message delivered here is that personal experience is valid unto itself.

However, the recurring and repetitive nature of these stories' themes exposes underlying issues such as racism, stereotyping, and underrepresentation upon which further research might shed light. To this end, each thematic section also includes a brief introduction that pulls together some of the scholarship that further documents and addresses the underlying causes for the stories' persistent occurrences.

Stories departs from existing literature in that it attempts to unravel and candidly reveal the socio-emotional experiences of being in front of the classroom, in labs, and in the ivory tower more generally. Each section is comprised of a series of letters followed by select commentaries from senior academics. By inviting seasoned scholars to submit guest commentaries, we mimic the format of most academic conferences by having a recognized, senior expert in the field draw conclusions or suggest additional questions for thought. The wide range of U.S. and internationally based scholars who have contributed their letters to the volume are referenced by name. However, several of our letter writers chose to remain anonymous or adopted pseudonyms to protect both their identities and their careers.

We hope that faculty of color, administrators, and members of the public will appreciate this book, as it provides an emotionally revealing window into a profession that remains virtually invisible to those outside the profession (and, as some of our contributors suggest, perhaps also to those in more privileged positions within the profession). Unlike the high-profile portrayals of doctors and lawyers in Western mainstream media, the everyday life of the professoriate remains shrouded in mystery. This book is a humble reminder that the academy, if not society at large, still wrestles with equality, even within a profession that positions intellectual honesty and academic freedom as its hallmarks.

Part I of the book includes letters focused on faculty of color's interactions with colleagues. The six letters address interactions ranging from the uplifting to the maddening. Specifically, contributors outline problematic encounters with senior faculty who believe that faculty of color have a deficit of credibility, share encouragement offered by mentors, and extend advice to junior academics on how to negotiate institutional politics. Dr. Al Young concludes this section with a view as an administrator.

Part II focuses on student-faculty interactions. Essays in this section highlight the problems, paradoxes, and possibilities within the teaching relationship. Touching and poignant, these letters speak to a core mission of the academy: to shape the young minds of future leaders in the context of personal and structural institutional hierarchies. Dr. Mary Pattillo provides an insightful essay about the importance of reflecting on one's own biases and privilege in the teacher-student dynamic.

The road to tenure is the primary topic of Part III. Letters in this section provide insight into a process that is often shrouded in mystery. These letters highlight how the demands of teaching, service, and research come together to impose unequal expectation of faculty of color. Dr. Juan Battle demystifies the process further with a mentor essay that provides advice for pre-tenured faculty.

Academic administration is the central theme of Part IV. This section is comprised of letters that outline the particular struggles faculty of color must navigate when working with representatives of the university's economic, political, and public relations interests. Several writers, including the mentor essay by Dr. Harvey Charles, provide strategies for navigating the administrative side of the academy.

The fifth and final part of the volume focuses on often-unspoken aspects of institutional climate. These essays address the topics that often go unmentioned—how racism permeates curriculum, academic (mis)recognition of scholars of color, faculty structure, and tenure expectations. Dr. Eduardo Bonilla-Silva poignantly reminds readers how to prioritize the variegated demands of a historically white-dominant professoriate in order to survive and thrive in the academy.

Together, these sections provide unparalleled insight into the lives of academics of color. We hope that the reader will gain a newfound appreciation for the often innovative and inspiring ways that faculty of color navigate complex social and institutional interactions that often mirror and magnify wider-society beliefs about inferiority and belonging as they enter the gates of their college campuses and take their place at the front of the room.

The single most pressing question that readers of this book might have is, "Why this volume *now*?" Haven't faculty of color experienced discrimination for a long time? Haven't their experiences been well-documented? The answer is yes: and yet, we believe that this volume is the first of its kind to represent the multifaceted nature of experiencing inclusion and exclusion in academia across a wide range of disciplines through personal stories.

Recent national news circuits have highlighted the countless challenges that contemporary faculty of color face in asserting their freedom of speech and in claiming a place of belonging within the academy. Social media movements such as the hashtag #ilooklikeaprofessor, aimed at challenging the expectation that college and university faculty fit a white, male, hetero-

normative mold, highlight the persistence of these social problems in a rapidly challenging 21st century, and the university as a central battleground for
what some are calling the neo–Civil Rights Movement known as Black Lives
Matter.

However, some months before racial conflicts on college campuses
erupted and were on the front page of national newspapers, we, the editors of
this volume, were piecing together letters from academics who could reflect
on the conditions that we were personally and collectively confronting in our
everyday experiences inside the "ivory tower." Below, as black faculty, each
of us provides personal vignettes on the winding and dizzying road leading to
the front of the room, how it has informed this collaborative project, and our
collective hope that the volume will provide courage and a road map for
colleagues who, too, remain in the trenches.

My stress levels were high. It was my first day of teaching. I walked into
the eighty-seat classroom at 2:49 p.m. as students from the previous course
were shuffling out of the room. As I walked in, I locked eyes with the
English professor whose class ended before mine. She looked me up and
down before finally looking me in the eye, and proceeded to roll her eyes in
complete disbelief and moderate disgust by what she had seen. I was a
young, female, light-skinned, black professor with her hair in locks. She was
a white, middle-aged, brown-haired and beige-toned woman, and my very
presence seemed to have soured her day.

I was simply too frazzled to address the initial impression of hostility. I
was preparing to deliver my first lecture to a classroom of 70 undergraduates
and I was, quite honestly, petrified. As I opened up my laptop and nervously
looked around for outlets, John, my department manager tried to help me get
situated.

"My class ends at 2:45," I heard in the distance.

I continued to shuffle my bag to grab my computer and notes. John was
five feet away from me organizing the technological connectivity I needed
for my lecture.

The voice repeated, "MY CLASS ENDS AT 2:45."

I looked to my left to figure out what was going on. The other professor
was looking at me from the side of her eye.

"Excuse me, I'm sorry. Are you talking to me?" I asked in a shaken voice.

She replied again, "My class ends at 2:45!" I later found out that the
professor believed that I entered the classroom too early. In her mind, I was
supposed to enter at 3 p.m., in order to give her more time to exit the
classroom.

I was stunned and confused. I tried to make sure the projector was con-
necting my computer so I could pull up my PowerPoint slides. John, visibly

uncomfortable, said, "Professor, this is Professor Clerge. She is teaching Quantitative Methods in this classroom after you and is trying to set up."

"I don't care who she is," she exclaimed. "My class ends at 2:45. I don't have all this stuff to set up. I just have my paper notes, and this small podium."

By this time, it was 2:55. Most of her students had trickled out of the room and mine were coming in. They, as well as my teaching assistant and research librarian, were witnessing what was happening and were also confused by this woman's claims. But the show had to go on. She later went to John, my department manager, and told him that he "should not be introducing me to her!"—referring to me. She told him, "You should be introducing her to me! I have twenty-five years more experience than that little girl will ever have." When I learned of this side conversation, I was blown away by this professor's rage. We had never crossed paths, and she knew nothing about me. All she knew was what she saw. I was a black female professor, decades younger than her, who seemed to be a part of social and technological changes that intimidated her.

On my first day as a fully naïve assistant professor, I rapidly went from being bright-eyed to feeling defeated by a fellow professor's public degradation of me in front of students, teaching assistants, and administrators. This was my introduction to the professoriate.

Even though I later received a forced apology from the professor stating, "I am sorry if I did something to offend you," nothing could address how mortified I was, and how it had compromised my sense of belonging at my university. Also, hindsight is 20/20. I know now that that incident sent me into a mild depression for two years. I felt uncomfortable in my skin. I never had the chance to settle into a new professorship without thinking about how my students and colleagues viewed me as an outsider within, an imposter, not smart or worthy enough. Not even deserving of compassion, let alone respect.

I was stripped of the opportunity to adjust to a new life, a new profession, a new city, and a new marriage as many of my white colleagues. Instead, confusion about my place in this predominantly white workspace and the surge in public attention to the rampant police killings of black girls and boys that gave way to the Black Lives Matter movement were the backdrop for my first year as a faculty member. I felt that the year could not end quickly enough.

I did not know who to turn to or what the proper course of action was. Other faculty members were baffled, and could only tell me "this never happens here." These well-intentioned individuals shared this "advice," believing that it was comforting. In fact, it only left me with the impression that the scarcity of new, junior, black, female faculty in a predominantly white institution meant that with my arrival, I had unwittingly become the catalyst for racial, gendered, and ageist conflicts.

In the midst of the confusion, I called on my network outside my institution. I spoke to my mentor, colleague, and friend Michelle Harris. I described my experience and we strategized about how to handle it. Before we got off the phone, Michelle said, "You know what? I've been meaning to work on a book with Sherrill that tells these stories, the war stories of faculty of color. I think that we can do something with this. We *should* do something with this."

—**Orly Clerge**

"Why this book?"

Why not?

Two thoughts immediately come to mind.

First, I cannot recall the singular moment that prompted my desire to become a Ph.D. Perhaps the seed was planted back in my undergraduate experience at Morehouse College, when for the first time I was inundated with the kind of black intellect that I never knew existed outside of a few essays written by Dr. W. E. B. Du Bois. I recall the respect I was taught to have for the "smartest" person in the room: the presumptive expert, with the Ph.D. degree that took a long time to *earn*. Although I graduated from Morehouse many moons ago, it pleases me that I am now in the privileged position of professor for many students, some of whom quietly draw strength from the fact that their image is finally reflected in front of the classroom.

Second, I distinctly recall a series of tough moments endured while en route in my quest to become a Ph.D. Part of the difficulty stemmed from the fact that I had already developed a life outside of academia. Balancing this life with my profession was not easy. My graduate program at Georgetown University would have posed a formidable challenge unto itself even if I were a single man. Yet I was not alone. During my graduate experience, I made the decision to do whatever was necessary to maintain a healthy marriage, with two young kids in tow. This is not the part where the reader reaches for tissue as their eyes begin to moisten. No, this is all merely to say that it took me a significant amount of time to reach the front of the classroom.

I do not take for granted my status within rarefied air.[1] Fewer than 6 percent of all history Ph.D.s are black like me (Racial/Ethnic Distribution of Degrees in History, 2016). Of that percentage, I am exceedingly sensitive that an even smaller percentage may be black males with tenure-track positions. Getting into graduate school, getting out of graduate school, and then getting into a tenure-track position were all struggles. Whether we blame the "market" or the "conspiracy," getting to the front of the classroom was a journey in and of itself. And this journey, with all its idiosyncrasies, is what this volume is about.

While I am fortunate to be gainfully employed, I am currently not professing at a historically black institution. In other words, my life's work is now directly situated inside of a predominantly (historically) white institution. What does this mean? Well, while I have fond memories of my desire to become a Ph.D. being sparked in part because I hoped to become inspiration for young people of color traditionally denied consistent access to higher education, most of my "clientele" are white students, colleagues, and administration. There's nothing wrong with this dynamic, per se. However, as aware as I am of the challenges I faced to reach my current position, the bottom line is that I personally have endured too much for too long to be disrespected without cause by uninformed and unexposed (mostly white) students who instinctively rebel without a cause, or who are quietly uncomfortable with the fact that their image is not represented in the features of their professor.

Or at least so they have been taught to think.

So yes, I dig deep into my bag of classroom management tricks and successfully connect with a good deal of students by semester's end, but the cycle of resistance is constant, consistent, and disconcerting.

The persistent marginalization of professors of color is common, symptomatic, and systematic.

It is also wrong and intellectually dishonest.

But I draw comfort in knowing I am not alone.

And so here we are.

Now it is time to be consistent and provide space for Ph.D.s of color to make their voices known in the quest for dignity and respect rightfully earned and wrongfully withheld.

My coeditors and I seek neither approval nor pity with this project. Rather, collecting these poignant, painful, and powerful stories is our contribution to both the change and continuity of racial struggle over time in this country . . . and, we hope our society's eventual evolution.

Why not?

—Frederick W. Gooding Jr.

I earned tenure and promotion in 2005 at a small, liberal arts institution in the Northeast. It was the 171st year of the institution's existence, yet I held the dubious distinction of being the first black person to obtain tenure. Other black faculty had been hired throughout the years, but none "survived"—the small town in which the school is located (or its small-town mindset), its isolated location, the reality of being the only black person on the faculty, or the overtly racist actions and rhetoric of some faculty colleagues—long enough to apply for tenure.

I survived. Not because I am a special snowflake, and not because I didn't "choke" (so said a colleague in my department when he explained why they hadn't hired a black person before me: "They look great on paper, but when we would bring them in to interview, they would just choke!"), but because I had a tremendous support system and an innate stubbornness; I survived.

I also survived by seeing in the faces of my students—regardless of race—the faces of my own children. In so doing, I acted toward them in the ways I wanted teachers and professors to act toward my five daughters—with respect, and caring, and the firm belief that hard work and determination could be more powerful than smarts alone.

The year I was offered that tenure-track job at the small college, the institution was successful in hiring four other black faculty members. Their dedication to racial diversification resulted from students' (mostly black students') protests about the fact that there was only one black person among the full-time faculty. My hire resulted in increasing the black faculty census by one hundred percent—at least for a few weeks. Shortly after this, the administration went all out and four other black colleagues, as well as five white ones, were hired. This was a big deal.

I know this was a big deal because a white colleague who was outraged about the "Affirmative Action hires" contacted *The Chronicle of Higher Education* and one of their reporters swooped in to tell the academic world about this rare phenomenon.

Thus, when the *Chronicle* ran the story titled "What Does It Mean When a College Hires 5 Black Scholars? Was it Luck, Determination, or a Change in the Rules?" many other folks in academia also asked those questions. Yes, I was featured, and yes, they even went so far as to reveal the credentials of the white versus the black candidates (path to degree, institution that granted the degree, etc.). Thus began my brief period of infamy; I was stopped twice in the supermarket in Ann Arbor by perfect strangers who asked me why I would choose to take a job at that college. I spent a lot of time that summer prior to my move hoping I had not made a wrong decision.

So why this book? Because there are, in fact, many stories that could have been written about my path to tenure and promotion and they are as least as traumatic as my *Chronicle* story. This book, however, represents to me the ability of faculty of color to not only survive similar situations—both public and private—but to resist oppressive structures and to offer a helping hand to others along the way. I hope it is another instance in which I can extend a hand to fellow *survivors* and *resisters* who needed to tell their stories; to feel validated in their perception of unfair treatment, overt racism, and microaggressions; and to join the survivors' club. It is also my way of staking a claim at the front of the room and assuring myself, my students, and my colleagues that I belong there as much as any other qualified "fronter."

—Michelle Harris

By way of background, I am a first-generation college student, graduate school student, and academic. This is important because I felt I did not know the "rules" of an academic career. I remember trying to describe tenure to my dad. His response: "Did you know this before you chose this job?!" Nope, didn't have a clue.

So I read everything (Kronenfeld and Strickland's 1993 *Getting Tenure* being one of my favorites), observed closely, and, quite honestly, benefited from unmerited kindnesses of mentors, friends, and sometimes near-perfect strangers. As I have learned the rules (both written and unwritten) I have been determined to share, to continue the legacy of lifting as we climb.

I am indebted to the sistah-scholars who have helped along the way and hope this volume carries that legacy forward. My initial tenure dossier was mediocre at best. I knew something was amiss but had no idea what needed to be done. My review committee thought it was "fine." One Thursday night, I found myself at a dinner for black women faculty and a senior woman noted that she heard I was going up for tenure and asked how it was going. I mentioned my dissatisfaction with and concern about the dossier, and she offered to read it.

Friday afternoon, I got an e-mail—"Please come to my office." She had read the dossier and had comments on every section. We spent five hours talking through the document. I remember being surprised that it was dark outside when I left to go home. Her words of wisdom—"This is a political document. What you see as strengths—collaboration and teamwork—others will read as a lack of independence and scholarly weight. Now is not the time to be modest. Rewrite with a focus on outcomes, on your intellectual contributions, and on the value of your work to the field. Your work—all of it—your research, your teaching, and your service—is important. Now make sure that everyone else knows it." Then she asked to see the rewrite, due to her by Sunday. That Monday morning I had a radically different dossier: one that got me tenure.

I wonder why others could not, or did not provide this type of feedback. Was it that my committee simply thought the initial version was the best I could do? Did they not see the weak case I was making? Did they not believe that the work, that my contributions as a teacher-scholar, were important? My committee was comprised of really good people—successful, respected scholars: people I considered allies. But they could not provide the critical feedback needed to move the dossier from modest and mediocre to strong, cogent, and confident.

In large measure, I owe my career to a sistah-scholar who generously gave much of her weekend to help someone she barely knew. In turn, I have read and commented on numerous dossiers, giving back a bit of what was given to me. But that's not enough. Individual efforts matter, but their reach is necessarily limited and they rarely can address the underlying causes.

Hence the importance of this volume, which describes the struggles faced by faculty of color, provides research evidence on the structures underpinning these occurrences, and presents strategies to address the issues the stories expose. We hope that sharing these stories—of heartbreak and healing—breaks silences, and breaking the silence of professors of color is an important step in creating the just classrooms to which we aspire. I hope the wisdom of those in this volume will resonate with faculty of color and their allies. Most important, I hope this volume provides faculty of color and their allies with strategies not simply to survive, but to thrive and to flourish.

—Sherrill Sellers

Thank you for joining us.
All our best,
Orly Clerge, Frederick Gooding Jr., Michelle Harris,
and Sherrill L. Sellers

REFERENCES

Antonio, A. 2002. "Faculty of Color Reconsidered: Reassessing Contributions to Scholarship." *Journal of Higher Education* 73(5): 582–602.

Joseph, T. and Hirshfield, L. 2011. "'Why Don't You Get Somebody New to Do It?' Race and Cultural Taxation in the Academy." *Ethnic and Racial Studies* 34(1): 121–41.

Racial/Ethnic Distribution of Degrees in History. 2016, April. http://www. humanitiesindicators.org/content/indicatordoc.aspx?i=251#fig255.

Stanley, C. 2006. "Coloring the Academic Landscape: Faculty of Color Breaking the Silence in Predominantly White Colleges and Universities." *American Educational Research Journal* 43(4): 701–36.

Turner, C.; González, J.; and Wood, J. 2008. "Faculty of Color in Academe: What 20 Years of Literature Tells Us." *Journal of Diversity in Higher Education* 1(3): 139–68.

Whicker, M.; Kronenfeld, J.; and Strickland, R. 1993. *Getting Tenure (Survival Skills for Scholars)*. Newbury Park, CA: Sage Publications.

NOTES

1. The proportion of doctorates awarded to blacks or African Americans has risen from 4.1 percent in 1994 to 6.4 percent in 2014, and the proportion awarded to Hispanics or Latinos has risen from 3.3 percent in 1994 to 6.5 percent in 2014. Source: National Science Foundation | National Center for Science and Engineering Statistics (NCSES). Doctorate Recipients from U.S. Universities: 2014.

I

Colleagues

Chapter One

Highlights of Research Literature on Colleagues and Faculty of Color

Can't Get No Respect

The cultural taxation that faculty of color endure in the academy may come from a variety of sources—including administration and student demands—but a good deal may also come from the stress inherent in negotiating professional relations with colleagues (Padilla, 1994; Joseph and Hirshfield, 2011). For generations, American colleges and universities used a culture of white supremacy legitimized by legislation to bar black, Mexican, Chinese, and Jewish people from both being admitted into and teaching on their campuses (Turner et al., 1999; Antonio, 2002). Half a century after the Civil Rights Movement, the professoriate continues to be predominately white and male, and faculty of color grapple with the legacy of their numerical and political marginalization in sharing daily tasks of research, teaching, and service with white colleagues.

Faculty of color confront the challenges of being both seen and unseen, living within the contradictions of the invisibility of their needs and values and their hypervisibility as racial "others" compared to their white colleagues. When faculty enter into a department, they are supposed to be socialized into the culture of the university, but also receive mentoring from senior faculty members who want to invest in their success on the tenure track.

Depending on the intersectionality of their experience (woman, bisexual, Muslim, immigrant, etc.), their varied treatment by fellow colleagues may be either a significant source of stress or a springboard for success. Many faculty of color who leave their universities do so because of toxic relationships

13

with their colleagues (Turner et al., 1999). From the first day that they step into their classrooms, their professional relations with colleagues are often characterized by isolation (being the "only one" in a department), the marginalization of "minority research" or researchers, and rebutting the beliefs of those who would cast them as "affirmative action babies" and not as qualified as a white faculty hire (Turner et al, 1999).

New faculty members enter into departments that before their arrival may be ambivalent about their hire. Attacks on affirmative action policy and widespread presumptions that faculty of color are underqualified may be reflected by the very colleagues with whom faculty of color share office space, socialize, and participate in department business. Like their white colleagues, faculty of color's hiring is voted upon by existing faculty members, and on "vote day," some of the most contentious personal and professional interests play into who gets hired and who doesn't.

Therefore, although faculty of color may earn a coveted faculty position, the departmental climate around their hire may have been fraught with tensions among existing faculty members. New faculty of any color may enter into a lion's den of department politics, where the feelings about their hiring are made abundantly clear through microaggressions, exclusionary tactics, or simple non-acknowledgment of their being "a part of the club" of existing faculty members.

Furthermore, the system of "training" that faculty experience is often spearheaded by the existing chair of the department. Faculty of color encounter a set of unique challenges in the relationship with their chairs. Because chairs are often mid-career or senior level faculty, they are more likely to be white men or women with little training in how to incorporate brown and black colleagues into a racially segmented professoriate. They may harbor their own discriminatory beliefs about the minority faculty or adopt a problematic color-blind stance.

Antonio (2002) finds that faculty of color make significant contributions to the scholarship of discovery and teaching and application. However, faculty of color are hired into departments and programs where they confront a culture that presumes a deficit of their credibility (Muhs et al., 2012). It's no surprise, then, that faculty of color often question their own ability to survive in and belong to their university.

As a result, faculty of color often are left to navigate the terrains of university politics, research, teaching, and service obligations on their own. Data has demonstrated that strong mentorship from a supportive senior colleague helps faculty "learn the ropes" and defend themselves against institutional problems. Because faculty of color are less likely to receive this mentorship (and sometimes don't know that they need it), they are locked out of important opportunities for learning, professional development, and personal growth.

Collegial relationships are also fruitful intellectual exchanges that may lead to internal research partnerships. However, research shows that faculty of color are more likely to encounter a "chilly climate" and are excluded from collaborative research opportunities that are presented to their white colleagues (Turner et al., 1999; Rockquemore and Laszloffy, 2008; Stanley, 2006). In their departments, there is often an insidious perception that their research and scholarship are not as rigorous as that of white faculty members, particularly if they work with communities of color. Although colleges and universities are believed to house liberal or progressive faculty who believe in the intellectual capacity and growth of students in a multiracial and multi-cultural society, implicit and explicit racial biases influence how white faculty assess their nonwhite faculty.

Faculty of color, therefore, have to negotiate the unrealistic expectation that they represent their racial or ethnic group through their above-average performance in teaching, research and service, and defying/shattering expectations of mediocrity. They note that their white colleagues often witness racism, sexism, and other forms of discrimination they face, but remain silent because of the perceived professional costs of speaking truth to power (Stanley, 2006).

In the same context, white faculty may use the race of their nonwhite peers as a resource in order to attract benefits to themselves or their departments through funding or diversity initiatives (Hirshfield and Joseph, 2012). Diversifying the professoriate becomes a commodity in the university's capitalistic operations. Faculty of color, then, become a bargaining chip whose humane, ethical, and intellectual contributions are only valued by an external incentive structure, not by a genuine interest in their scholarly or pedagogical contributions.

The letters in this section of *Stories from the Front of the Room* describe the inherent complications of collegiality in racially unequal academic settings. Harris and Prieto Langarica's coauthored vignettes uncover the ways in which white colleagues interpret their "Mexicanness" through their names, credentials, and potential – often at first sight. In a letter addressed to his colleagues, Oware, too, describes an indignant confrontation with a senior white colleague during a department meeting. Oware elucidates the often-times contentious nature of faculty relations, and the retaliation experienced by faculty of color who speak up and state their opinions during ostensibly collaborative faculty meetings.

Similarly, Hopeful's essay demarcates the challenges she faces as a first generation Latina woman of color in a STEM field. In a letter addressed to her mentor, Hopeful seeks advice on how to navigate the unprofessional nature of her interactions with her colleagues. The encounter Hopeful's letter describes centers around a "critic," a white female senior colleague in a department meeting, and is fraught with insults to her authority and more shockingly, questions concerning her qualifications as an assistant professor of mathematics.

Wilder's letter draws our attention to the hostility of informal networking spaces. While faculty meetings may be more obvious sites of tension over power, off-campus social gatherings of faculty can also be problematic spaces for faculty of color, who may continue to be assaulted with micro- and macroaggressions alike from colleagues and administrators, even in their precious "free time."

Wilder addresses an incident when a white colleague exclaimed that black people like her should have "no more excuses" for complaints after the election of Barack Obama. Mortified by the incident, Wilder vividly outlines the ways she has found she has to address the continuous assaults on her professional worth, even outside of an institution's walls.

The Patient Professor's essay concludes this section on collegiality (or the lack thereof) with portraits both of how students interpret faculty of color in relation to their white colleagues and the condescending nature in which other faculty members respond to the opinions of faculty of color, particularly women. Patient Professor's encounter with a "hugger" who addressed her comments in a professional meeting with an unprofessional hug was only exacerbated when a female colleague ignored her request for privacy in addressing the situation by publicizing the incident on campus without her permission.

Whether it's in a parking lot where white faculty interpret one as an outsider and call the authorities, or at dinner parties in colleagues' homes, the subtle and blatant struggles for respect and legitimacy are the additional "tax" faculty of color must pay when they join the "club."

REFERENCES

Antonio, A. 2002. "Faculty of Color Reconsidered: Reassessing Contributions to Scholarship." *Journal of Higher Education* 73(5): 582–602.

Hirshfield, L. and Joseph, T. 2012. "'We Need a Woman, We Need a Black Woman': Gender, Race, and Identity Taxation in the Academy." *Gender and Education* 24(2): 213–27.

Joseph, T. and Hirshfield, L. 2011. "'Why Don't You Get Somebody New to Do It?' Race and Cultural Taxation in the Academy." *Ethnic and Racial Studies* 34(1): 121–41.

Muhs, G. G.; Niemann, Y. F.; González, C. G.; and Harris, A. P. (eds.). 2012. *Presumed Incompetent: The Intersections of Race and Class for Women in Academia.* Boulder: University Press of Colorado.

Rockquemore, K. and Laszloffy, T. 2008. *The Black Academic's Guide to Winning Tenure—Without Losing Your Soul.* Boulder: Lynne Rienner Publishers.

Stanley, C. 2006. "Coloring the Academic Landscape: Faculty of Color Breaking the Silence in Predominantly White Colleges and Universities." *American Educational Research Journal* 43(4): 701–36.

Turner, C.; Myers Jr., S.; and Creswell, J. 1999. "Exploring Underrepresentation: The Case of Faculty of Color in the Midwest." *The Journal of Higher Education* 70(1): 27–59.

Chapter Two

Letters

Dear Fellow Underrepresented Junior Faculty Members,

We are two Hispanic female mathematicians with a common experience in the academy: walking into a room and seeking people like us. Often we are the only women and/or minorities in the room. Searching for a sense of belonging while pursuing higher education and a professional career as academics, particularly in a white male–dominated field like mathematics, can be emotionally draining. It makes us feel isolated. These feelings are exacerbated when we experience additional challenges due to our status as minorities. This includes dealing with negative racial comments or more subtle microaggressions.

Like many students, we believed these incidents would end as we achieved our goal of completing a doctoral degree. We both discovered, that is not always the case. Here are two illustrative stories dealing with some of our negative experiences.

Pamela's Story: A Nightmare Job Interview

As I was completing my Ph.D. in the early part of 2012, I flew to Boston for the annual Joint Mathematics Meeting (JMM), the largest gathering of mathematicians in the United States. I was thrilled to attend my first JMM, and I had many initial job interviews lined up. I had high hopes for the prospects these meetings could develop.

Job interviews are reminiscent of speed dating. The candidates wait in a large room while members of search committees sit at tables in an exhibit hall. Once called, there's just enough time to say hello and for the committee to ask about your research, your teaching, and sometimes even what you do for fun. Twenty to thirty minutes later, you say goodbye and return to the waiting area for the next interviewer to call your name.

My infamous interview began when the male interviewer waiting at the table was completely surprised to see me. This, I deduced a minute later, was due to the fact that I look Hispanic yet have an American-sounding name. His first question: "So, is your dad white and your mom Mexican?" I told him that both of my parents were Mexican, at which point he proceeded to point at my name tag and then at my face, while telling me he was confused about my name. I explained to him that I am Mexican and took my African American husband's name.

I wish the story ended there, but unfortunately it only got worse. The complete version includes his comments on how minorities do not learn mathematics because it is a "cultural issue." The utter shock of what I was experiencing paralyzed me. Instead of screaming and flipping tables over (which always raises ratings), I walked out of the large hall and called my husband. My worst nightmare came true: even with a Ph.D., I was not accepted or recognized as a mathematician.

Alicia's Story: Finding Respect in the Classroom

Gaining the respect of our students through our teaching is paramount to their learning, but student disrespect is something that I have experienced since I began my career as a professor. Being a young, Hispanic, woman mathematician, I have learned that my relaxed teaching style is conducive to student learning, as the students feel more comfortable asking math questions or making teachable mistakes. However, this style of teaching has also proven to have the disadvantage that students find it hard to see me as an authority figure.

Take for example a past summer calculus class when I had a particularly difficult time dealing with a student who I'll call Jane. I always explain to students that, for most, the difficulties in calculus stem from the challenges of algebra. As I do with all of my calculus classes, I asked the students in Jane's class to come to office hours if they needed help with algebra concepts. Even after these comments, Jane consistently interrupted my lecture to ask algebra questions, to which I would respond, "That is a great question, but since it is an algebra question, do you mind asking during office hours?" On one occasion, she responded by stating, "I am paying you to be here and to teach me this during class." From this point on her interactions with me became extremely hostile, and she made it a point to aggressively question all algebraic steps during class lectures.

One particular day things escalated quickly. She walked into my office, where a student was working out a problem on the board. She slammed her quiz down on my desk and yelled, "I don't understand why you took points off on this question!" I calmly explained that there was a student in my office, and I asked her to please wait outside while I finished working with that student.

Her response: "I pay you to have office hours for me, so you have to pay attention to me!" I proceeded to tell her: "So does he," as I pointed at the other student in my office, "so please step outside and wait your turn." Jane became very upset and started yelling: "You have something personal against me, and I don't even care that you are Mexican!" We both stood in silence while the other student turned around in disapproval. I was unsure what she meant with that comment, so I asked her: "What does my being Mexican have to do with anything?" She became very defensive and left my office. In fact, she never again attended my office hours, and I believe she finally figured out that her issue with me was my heritage.

Many negative experiences of faculty of color are not as obviously discriminatory as those we presented. These smaller, yet still negative, experiences are often referred to as microaggressions, and unfortunately, these are a more common experience faced by faculty of color. Microaggressions are just as detrimental to our self-identity as professors. What follows are a few examples:

- I once covered a class for a colleague, and at the end of the class a white male faculty member, whom I had never met, was next to teach in that classroom. He approached me and asked me to make sure I cleaned and washed the boards. In his mind, I was not a professor, but instead the custodian.
- People always assume that the accomplishments of a minority faculty member are due to some affirmative action policy and have nothing to do with merit. Recently, I was told by one of my male colleagues that of course I was going to be granted tenure: after all, I *am* a Hispanic woman.
- Whenever there is a meeting and food is present, I am the one expected to help serve and clean afterward, without fail.
- Students feel entitled to question your authority or your qualifications. Once, a student asked me: "What are your credentials to teach this class?"

Finding positive ways to deal with racism, sexism, and the sense of insecurity that these and myriad other smaller incidents produce is paramount as we proceed in our academic careers. By trial and error, and with a little bit of luck, we have found ways to build a supportive network of peers and mentors who help each other develop a sense of belonging. We share these tips with you in the hope that you too can build your supportive network and thrive in academia.

- Find other faculty of color. The struggles faced by faculty of color in academia are not restricted to a particular discipline. Supportive peers with whom you feel safe sharing stories and advice will keep you sane and even laughing as you move forward in your career.
- Find supportive mentors in and outside of your institution. Having someone who can give you career advice is important, especially as you are navigating through the tenure process.
- Organize a speaker series. Our co-organized speaker series has allowed us to bring possible collaborators to our institutions. Additionally, inviting speakers from diverse backgrounds allows students to meet and interact with other minority researchers.
- Become a faculty advisor for a student organization. Not only will you get to work with students, but you are also helping future generations by being the mentor they need. You may even get service points toward tenure.
- Attend conferences. If diversity is hard to find on your campus, look outward. For those in STEM fields, the Society for Chicanos/Hispanics and Native Americans in Science (SACNAS) holds a great national conference, where you can find friends, mentors, and collaborators, all while enjoying a sense of cultural community unlike any other scientific conference in the nation.

Our stories only scratch the surface of the experience of being a woman of color in a STEM field. The challenges will span your academic career and having a Ph.D. or even tenure may not eliminate them. But remember, although our community might be small in numbers, it is close and strong. We hope that the strategies we shared help you find a sense of belonging. And we end by reminding you that the one thing you can be certain of is that, no matter how challenging things get, you belong here!

Sincerely,
Pamela E. Harris, Davies Research Fellow, United States Military Academy, and Alicia Prieto Langarica, Assistant Professor, Youngstown State University

LETTER 2

Dear Colleagues,
I suppose I should apologize.
Again.
I honestly did not realize that when I openly, but innocently, suggested that we maintain our standards when assessing job candidates for our new teaching position I would be yelled and screamed at—"I AM NOT LOWER-

ING MY STANDARDS"—by our senior white colleague. As I sat there mortified during our departmental meeting, I wondered what was happening. Why was this person literally shouting at me? Should I say something? How should I respond, as standing chair of the department? As we all listened to our colleague—aghast in stunned silence—after a minute or so, I calmly interrupted the rant by saying this person's first name.

Surprisingly, I was shouted down. "NO, YOU LISTEN! I AM NOT LOWERING MY STANDARDS . . . AND YOU." At this point, I realized this would not stop unless someone else spoke up or I raised my voice. I was acutely aware of the consequences of adding volume to my voice. I would be characterized as one of the worst epithets in academia for a person of color— the angry black man. Not wanting that, I looked down at my folders, as the outburst continued, and calmly said, "I am done." Indeed, I had covered everything necessary in the meeting. So, I gathered my documents, rose from my seat, and left the room.

As you may know, this colleague followed me into my office wanting to speak with me. I felt forced to honor the demand of "talking" at that moment. Still bewildered from the department meeting, I quickly asked another senior-level colleague to join us in my office. Person X initially offered a half-hearted apology, but then proceeded to tell me many of my wrongdoings, stating that their only intent throughout my time as chair was to do what was best for the department. You may not know that two years before I became chair I met with this colleague (and, again, another senior-level colleague) to discuss another issue—at that time this individual told me that I seemed "angry."

After the post-departmental meeting with the "ranter," it was suggested that I send out an e-mail stating that we apologize for what occurred. Let me be clear, I do not have any remorse for advocating that we uphold our standards for all candidates. Briefly, my election as chair of the department happened during a critical juncture: there were several retirements on the horizon, we were discussing major curricular changes, and we had just had an external review of the department. I am proud that many of you felt that I was the right person to address these concerns. Indeed, I am the first person of color who has served as chair; I fully appreciate its significance.

Our external review pointed out several areas of improvement with "low morale" of junior faculty being one of the greatest concerns in my mind. At that time, I was untenured and privy to conversations with other junior colleagues regarding morale. Several felt that they were not allowed a voice in the department and that some senior colleagues dominated conversations around important issues. As the new chair, I sought to provide multiple opportunities for these individuals to be heard. However, as my own story illustrates, that was easier said than done.

I realized that our colleague's outburst created an uneasiness in the department; thus, after I sent out the apologetic e-mail to the department, I personally talked to just about everyone to address the situation and reassure all that I would serve out my chairship and tackle the issues raised in the external review.

Frankly, it was moments like these when I actually considered stepping down. At times it felt overwhelming and exhausting, especially from those who did not support—or showed outright hostility toward—me. But, I remained undeterred, confident that I would not let others dictate my actions or silence me. Indeed, I felt support from those who stated that there was not a need for *me* to apologize—I was *not* the person in the wrong.

As I analyze our colleague's behavior I came to the realization that my comment was viewed as a challenge or threat to this person's sense of entitlement, more precisely, X's white privilege. Here I am, this younger, black, male, junior colleague daring to speak his mind. I stepped out of my place and needed to be reprimanded where all could see and understand. My query was an affront to white authority that had already identified me as unfit for the position as chair—and "angry" on top of that. I later found out that this characterization had been expressed to fellow colleagues and even our university president.

In response, I met with our president (a benefit of working at a small liberal arts institution), requesting the opportunity to reply to my critics. I am not sure if this meeting changed the way I was defined.

In my mind, Colleague X's outburst illustrates the insidiousness of white privilege—it can, and often does, present itself as objective, innocuous, and legitimate, remaining hidden and unrecognizable even in plain view. Of course, we know this from the scholarship in this area. However, many people of color in academia recognize it at a personal level—my example, when a white colleague can, with impunity, yell and berate me. It was not a microaggression, but an act of aggression!

Despite this occurrence, I agreed to serve as chair of the department for a second term. This is only because of the immense support I received during my previous term. I thank you all for the countless supportive conversations and e-mails, the pats on the back, and the genuine encouragement. Although I was told this was a thankless job—oddly enough, by the person who screamed at me—I am very appreciative of colleagues who believed and backed me at key times when important decisions were made. I enjoyed the laughs and light-hearted moments I shared with most of you.

Now, I am in my last year as chair. It is somewhat less tumultuous; we don't walk around on eggshells. However, I think tension still remains. The "ranter" and I are cordial, but speak infrequently. Sadly, this is the resolution to the situation. As a department, though, we managed to address major concerns and accomplished what we needed to over these six years—made talented and strong new hires, provided more venues and opportunities for our students to present their research, and strengthened our curriculum, among other changes. Multiple colleagues were recipients of teaching awards, and published books, book chapters, and journal articles. Several of our students went on to graduate and professional school, or obtained meaningful jobs. We have made great strides.

I do not envy the person who follows me. There remains much important work that needs to be done. I hope she or he will not have to face some of the problems I have encountered. Candidly, I believe the next chair may have an easier time if male and white. A historical inertia exists whereby this particular identity readily receives legitimacy and status in our profession. However, we are making slow advancements. Growing numbers of people of color in academe are coming through the pipeline. I hope we benefit from this growth.

Nevertheless, I again apologize. But know that even as my term as chair ends, I will keep fighting the necessary fight for my departmental colleagues and people of color. I just have to shake off the haters!

Sincerely,
Matthew Oware
Associate Professor and (outgoing) Chair
Sociology and Anthropology
DePauw University

LETTER 3

Dear Mentor,

I am turning to you once more for guidance and reassurance. Now that I am a new tenure-track faculty member in this mathematics department I am having a very difficult time figuring out how to be around a fellow faculty member—a person I'll call "the critic." There have been several interactions with the critic that have left me disheartened, discouraged, and made me question whether or not I am qualified to be here.

Of course, I have been doing what I usually do in these situations— perhaps what many of us underrepresented people do—thinking, "Am I reading too much into it?" I guess I did not reach out to you earlier about these encounters because I continued to ask myself that question. Also, I know that if I talked to you about it, you would be hearing only my side. I figured you would tell me what Pee Wee Reese told Jackie Robinson, "You know, Jack, some of these guys are throwing at you because you're black. But others are doing it just because they plain don't like you." So I have never allowed myself to ask if it stems from my being a woman, an underrepresented

minority, or because they don't view my research as being rigorous enough.
Until now.

The very first time I met the critic during my on-campus interviews I felt
uncomfortable. Even then, their introduction included an explanation to me
regarding their seniority in the department and how they were a serious
researcher (unlike everyone else?). During my presentation, the critic asked,
"This is your *Ph.D. research*?" Perhaps they were not informed that the
candidates were asked to make their talks accessible to the undergraduate
population.

Throughout my visit to campus, I learned of the great initiatives the
university is involved in that serve the community and its diverse student
body. I felt elated that I had found a university whose vision is in line with
my values. However, in conversations with the critic I learned that they did
not feel that these values have merit.

I decided not to let this person's opinions shatter my views of the department and university as a whole and accepted my job offer. I was humbled
when this institution hired me as their first Latina, STEM, tenure-track faculty to join the math department. I thought that the landscape of higher education was progressing since the president of the institution was excited to hire
one of only 52 Latinas in the US who received Ph.D.s in STEM that year
(only a fraction of those pursue a career as academics).

During the first few weeks of the semester I had forgotten about my
conversations with the critic. It helped a lot that I did not see them, for the
most part—they are rarely on campus. However, even the shortest encounters
would leave me feeling downhearted. I gave a more extensive research talk
on some ongoing work to our mathematics department faculty and senior
level students.

The critic walked in as I had finished my talk, just as the audience was
asked if they had any questions. The critic raised their hand and jokingly
asked what the talk was about. This was entirely inappropriate. I pondered
what the students in the audience might think of our department and what
examples of respect among peers we were showing them. I definitely never
saw anything like this before. I was taught to value and thank a speaker for
taking their time to share their research. I tried telling myself that maybe this
person was trying to be playful, but considering our interactions, I find it
unacceptable. In fact, other colleagues in my department validated my feelings.

This week we had a departmental meeting in which we discussed the
math department's new faculty search. The critic immediately expressed how
disappointed they were with the previous search. I sat there staring straight at
them, not believing what was coming out of their mouth.

As soon as the critic started talking I noticed that my colleagues let them
speak with minimal interruption and after some time I noticed all my col-

leagues' eyes were distant. I tried this tactic of tuning them out for a moment but instead decided to really listen. I heard that in the previous search, the one in which I was hired, there were strong arguments within the search committee regarding who received the on-campus invitation and the final job offer.

The implication was that I was hired because I am a Latina and, while the other candidates had some desirable qualities, they did not make it because they are not Latino. At this point I had an emotional reaction because the critic was basically telling me that it was not my qualifications that got me this job, but my ethnicity. How should I have reacted in that situation?

I know this person is wrong. I am the right fit for what my department and this university needs. I am a proof-by-example that there is a place for Latina mathematicians in higher education. In my faculty role, I am faced with a diverse student body looking to me with eager eyes and hoping I will be their role model. I have established a strong rapport with my students and I have their trust. I am here to help students of a diverse background navigate this confusing landscape. The story I tell them belongs to a young, first-generation Latina whose co-star is you, my mentor. Your guidance and persistence have complemented my best qualities and have prepared me for what awaits me as a senior scholar.

After only one year in my current position, I am really beginning to value your effort and dedication. You have watched me, guided me, and helped me navigate the academic landscape. When I felt there was no place for a Latina among mathematicians, you reminded me that not seeing any does not imply that we don't belong. You understand that improvement is needed with regard to how minority groups are educated in mathematics, and that in order to do so, the faculty population needs to be broadened to include persons of diverse backgrounds. You saw my potential and believed in my abilities and in my desire to improve myself. After all, don't I have the right to strive for the American Dream?

For so long, I have been under-represented and underestimated in higher education. You have always been honest. You told me my math knowledge had gaps, and you showed me how to fill them. More importantly, you always reminded me that I had the ability to fill these gaps and to keep having confidence in myself. All the experiences you presented me—research, talks, travel—have brought me to this point, and I feel confident. And here I am, thanks to you.

I want to join you and follow your example. Without a doubt, it has taken a lot of effort on both of our parts and more than ever, I am grateful to you. Thank you, Mentor. I made it this far and I can see the career-long effort you have made toward making math education accessible: I am energized. I realize now that you have had to deal with many critics like my colleague. I feel optimistic as I take on this role, but hope you will continue to guide me.

This leaves me wondering: how do I approach the critics and my fellow faculty colleagues who do not see that although we have made improvements at my institution (in spite of the critics) there is still so much work to be done on a national scale?

I am here to carry your legacy and follow your lead. I have the advantage of knowing what worked for me and helped me break through an invisible barrier that exists for so many Latinos. I can't do it alone; I need more advocates like you to join this cause. When I was confronting so many difficult hurdles, you urged me to remain persistent and overcome the challenges I faced.

My critic is my new challenge and I will continue to turn to you for strength and guidance. I know that together we will overcome many critics. With your support, I have been successful and I won't back down when faced with them. My story is evidence that with more mentors like you, we can be successful moving forward and continue our progress toward making math education fair and accessible.

Yours truly,
Hopeful

LETTER 4

Dear Colleague,

You probably don't remember me. And to be quite honest, if I were to walk past you on campus today, I would not recognize you either. Ironically, our inability to point each other out in a crowded room of our faculty colleagues is exactly how color-blind racism, white privilege, and white denial operates today. Some whites, who are in denial of their privilege, can't see or recognize their racist practices. People of color, who all too often have to deal with and work through racial microaggressions on a regular basis, try hard to forget. While the faces and names attached to racialized moments may soon leave us, the memory of the emotions connected to the event *never* fades.

That said, I will never forget the day that we met. It was November 4, 2008—Election Day. I was several weeks into my first semester as a new professor, and I was still quite nervous about my first job on the tenure track. I was at the time (and remain today) the only African American faculty person in my department, and I was trying hard to adjust to my new position at a predominately white university.

A mutual colleague of ours invited me to her home that evening to watch the return of the votes. At first, I was not interested in going, but then on second thought, I decided to attend. I was beginning to understand the informal rules of collegiality, and recognized that my failure to attend a social event off-campus could impact me negatively later on. Or at least that is what I was taught by my mentors of color who had warned me about the unwritten rules of faculty politics within higher education.

I arrived at our colleague's home around 7 p.m., and was greeted with a warm welcome by a group of fellow faculty members and several graduate students. I made my way into the living room and sat down across from you. You looked at me, and gave me a friendly smile. I introduced myself to you and we began to chat.

In my mind, I started to feel more comfortable, and thought that coming to this party wasn't such a bad idea after all.

The election results came in earlier than expected, and it was announced that Barack Obama was elected the 44th President of the United States, making history as the first black commander in chief.

Everyone at the party began celebrating. While I was overjoyed, I was hesitant to express my true feelings of euphoria because I was not surrounded by any of my close friends or family members. I was in a state of disbelief thinking about the enormity of the moment.

You jolted me back to reality, however, when you looked at me, pointed your finger in my face and said, "No more excuses."

"Obama is president now, so no more excuses."

You went on to "encourage" me to get my education. You asked that I share this message of uplift with my brothers, cousins, and everyone I knew because there were no more excuses *now*.

I stared at you in amazement, stood up, and walked away. Startled by your insensitive remarks, I decided to excuse myself from the party and go home.

I was so angry at you for your blatant ignorance, arrogance, and racism (and undoubtedly, your sexism and ageism, too). I don't know why you felt that you had me, my life, my family and my educational background all figured out within five minutes of meeting me. I don't understand how you missed the biggest part of our small talk when I shared with you that I was new to the university. While I never openly stated that I was a new professor, I assumed that it was implied. I certainly assumed that *you* were.

When I got home that evening, I was so disappointed in myself for letting your actions go unchecked. I wanted to find you on campus the next day and tell you how wrong you were about me. I wanted to correct you and to show you that we were actually colleagues—that just like you, I had earned my doctorate and my credentials were impeccable. I wanted to tell you that my family—like many African American families—already knows the value of an education (in fact, I am a third generation Ph.D.). We don't need random white folks admonishing us to go to school and lecturing on the importance of learning because we have been taught this by our own communities from an early age.

But I never looked for you the next day. I decided that it wasn't worth it. I didn't want to risk my future as scholar of color at my new institution. Quite frankly, I was afraid to call you out on your actions for fear of reprisal.

Even further, I am certain that had I confronted you the next morning about your racial insensitivity, you would have denied your actions, and framed your behavior within the context of good will and unintentionality. You would have reminded me that you voted for Obama, and that you were excited about his historic victory, just like me. You may have even tried to tell me about your other faculty colleagues of color, or perhaps even the students of color that you may have mentored over the years as a way to dismiss *my* misunderstanding of what occurred the night before. You may have even blamed your slip of the tongue on your glass of wine.

I decided instead to focus my efforts and energy on why I was in the academy in the first place. When I joined the professoriate, I looked forward to being a mentor and guide to all of my students, but most notably, to the ones who looked like me. Inside and outside the classroom, I utilize my position as a young, black, female professor as my daily opportunity to create awareness, to dispel the negative, one-dimensional stereotypes of black womanhood, and to challenge students (and colleagues) to broaden their horizons about what they think blackness is or should be.

And here we are seven years later, nearing the end of President Obama's second term. I have earned tenure now, and I am much more comfortable in my skin. In thinking back on the first time we met, I must take this opportunity to let you know, my faculty colleague, that I am no longer afraid.

I am penning this letter—for myself and for the many others who remain silenced and afraid—as a figurative finger in the face of the academy: no more excuses, now. Today, in the midst of the Obama Era, black women are attaining doctoral degrees (and other educational degrees, for that matter) at *higher* rates than any other group of women in America. We are outpacing and trendsetting in many areas beyond education, including the media, business, and politics. In case you haven't noticed, we have three generations of black women living at 1600 Pennsylvania Avenue.

No more excuses, now. Allow me to educate you.

On a regular basis, many black academics and other faculty of color have to question their belonging and fit in a place that often deems them inferior. The tax of being an underrepresented minority in a world that blatantly and inadvertently questions your value, fit, and legitimacy can at times be downright exhausting.

Over the years, the emotional work of processing even the smallest slight from a student or colleague has left me wondering if I am being hypersensitive and over dramatic. And this is precisely the reason why many faculty of color, and especially women of color, decide to leave (or are even forced out of) the academy altogether.

Dear colleague, there are no more excuses for racism in the academy—no matter how polite, subtle, blind, and unintentional your version may be. While we are living in the post–civil rights era with a black president and countless other people of color in positions of authority and power, racism continues to permeate every institution in American society, particularly higher education.

And the most insidious form of racism is perpetuated by people like you who are in denial of your privilege and your propensity to be racist—in spite of being surrounded by people of color on a regular basis, at work, at home, and at social gatherings.

I no longer have anything to prove to you and the many other folks like you that I have encountered along the way who don't give me the courtesy or benefit of my hard-earned faculty status. I don't need your validation anymore.

I look like a professor just as much as you do.

I belong here.

Tell everyone you know. No more excuses, now.

Your Colleague,
JeffriAnne Wilder, Ph.D.

LETTER 5

Dear Nicole, (or, A Note to Nicole on Becoming Tax-Free)

I can only imagine how much of a surprise it will be for you to receive this letter, but since I'm putting together my tenure file, there seemed like no better occasion to write. You were part of the last class of graduating high school seniors I got to teach before I "retired" to start a doctoral program at a school eight hours away. Remember how you and some of the other young black women in your class laughed at me for using that term? *Retirement is for old people,* you all said, certainly not a woman in her late twenties. I met your laughter with a question: *How can I teach you all to chase your dreams if I don't chase my own?*

In the decade that has passed since that conversation, I've realized how much the experience of teaching African American and women students like you, shaped me. Now that you're finishing your graduate degree, I can confess that a small piece of me wants to think your choice to teach comes from the same commitments that inspired me to chase my dream.

Unfortunately, I didn't know that commitments like these can set you up to fail when I began my career as a professor. The failure that changed me happened during the spring of my first year on the tenure track. I was a newly minted Ph.D., eager to try out my pedagogical techniques and all too aware that I was the first African American, tenure-track, English professor in my small, Southern, liberal arts school's history.

Despite my feelings about that, I realized that one of the school's best assets was its racially diverse student body population. At no other institution where I have taught has there been so many African American and Native American students, so I turned my attention to them and began to work on designing courses that would resonate with them. This strategy was working well enough for me that Professor A, one of the senior faculty in my department, invited me to give the guest lecture for the session of his Film and Literature course devoted to the adaptation of Alice Walker's *The Color Purple* after visiting one of my Black Women Writers class sessions to observe my teaching.

He knew that I had taught the novel and film earlier that semester, and explained in his e-mail that he thought I would be a great guest to talk about the controversy among African American audiences around the film's release. He also noted that my students had engaged in a rigorous discussion on stereotypical images of black women in contemporary media when he visited. How could I say no? He seemed to appreciate my teaching style, so I set out to plan a similar lesson that lived up to the honor of his request.

Any sense of honor evaporated as my lecture progressed. Professor A.'s class was twice the size of mine and far less diverse. There were only three African American students of thirty, but they greeted me warmly along with the rest of the students. At first, the majority of the class expressed interest as I explained how I use film and television to show how rhetoric teaches us to understand race and representation, and they seemed to appreciate my opening activity of discussing the then-recently released film adaptation of *The Hunger Games,* as an example of how coming-of-age literature teaches readers to understand the world.

Once I shifted the conversation to the controversy about the film producer's choice to cast major African American actors in the role of major characters, the resistance began. Vocal students started to make defensive statements as I showed the largely racist social media tweets of fans complaining about the film's casting. Some became audibly defiant when I asked the class to think about what those social media messages might mean about how the public is conditioned to view people of color. At one point I overheard a white male student sigh heavily and say, "Oh, I see how this is going to go."

Even the small group of students that were still talking grew reticent when I shifted to the next stage of my lecture to focus on the history of negative images of black women in popular film that might have made viewers skeptical of the film *The Color Purple.* As I projected film and television images of black women who seemed to conjure up tropes like "the mammy" and "the jezebel" and asked them to unpack some of the assumptions and attitudes those images invoke, the already tense atmosphere of my class thickened.

It was only when I noticed that the three young black women in the class were visibly embarrassed that I decided to make some final remarks about stereotypes, representation, and the worry around what message Walker's film would send when it came out. After a quick wrap-up, I grabbed my computer and walked out, passing Professor A who was standing quietly at the back of the class, and left. I had never felt like such a failure before.

My embarrassment lingered for days. Was the lesson too provocative? Had I assumed too much about the students' ability to think critically about media and themselves? Had I been insensitive to the class dynamics? These questions were the soundtrack to the images of those embarrassed, young, black women that circulated in my mind. After I realized that I had made the best decisions with the information I had, I thought about the work I put in. Resentment followed. Finally, I broke down and told another first-year professor about my failed visit over lunch.

"Based on the students' reactions when I began that conversation about race, you'd think they had never talked about any of those issues before," I said. "How do you teach black women's writing without any lead-in work? It's like Professor A had not prepped them for the topic or my visit at all."

Without blinking, my colleague turned and said, "He didn't have to. That's what you were there to do."

That conversation changed how I teach and work. As you may know, the pull toward "respectability," or the socially and sometimes internally dictated obligation African Americans feel to always show their most dignified selves to the public, is strong and it can start early for black women.

Even when I resist respectability's stranglehold on the content I teach, it still shapes the communities I hope to reach most through my teaching, so I already feel like I fret more about teaching than most. Given the additional labor these levels of concern create, the kinds of "cultural taxation" Audrey Williams June describes in her *The Chronicle of Higher Education* article "The Invisible Labor of Minority Professors" become even worse for scholars of color. As she explains, universities are so racially homogenous that minority students flock to minority faculty members to fulfill their therapeutic, mentoring, and advocacy needs.

While these faculty members are more apt to feel invested in the academic success and emotional wellness of these students, these expectations manifest as a kind of rent, or "cultural taxation," to create a space for themselves and students that may look like them or share their experiences in the academy. The cost is high. Already underrepresented faculty end up devoting intellectual and emotional labor to helping students at a time when they must also produce high-quality research and demonstrate exemplary teaching. And faculty within dominant groups let them or expect them to because they assume African Americans, women, Latino/a, or LGBTQ faculty are better equipped to do this work.

In this light, Nicole, you'll need to declare yourself "tax-free" if you plan to embark on an effective and sustaining teaching career that serves the communities I believe you want to reach. Even if my colleague was off-base in her analysis of that class and Professor A simply wanted to expose his students to a style of teaching that he admired, the assumptions that make "cultural taxation" such a burden also creates a dangerous form of negligence.

I retired from this kind of work when I realized that even with my good intentions and work, I am likely to wound myself as well as the students I care about in needless ways if I don't start to question the assumptions and labor politics of my department. I had to learn to release myself from the expectation that I could be perfect within conditions I have not created. Ultimately, I had to let go of the assumption that I alone could fill glaring curricular potholes. I am tax-free now because I know that *doing* diversity well is everyone's work.

Free yourself, dear. You can still do world-changing work, but you have to be present to do so.

All my best,
Prof. Carey

REFERENCE

June, A. W. 2015. "The Invisible Labor of Minority Professors." http://chronicle.com/article/ The-Invisible-Labor-of/234098.

LETTER 6

To My Esteemed Colleagues and Inquisitive Students,

I have always wanted to teach, but it was only after attending engineering school that my desire to educate transitioned from the high school to the collegiate level. Although I know that teaching is my gift and that I am walking out my destiny every day, there were some aspects of the profession that I was not prepared for. The lack of diversity in the science, technology, engineering and math (STEM) fields is just one example. My choice to teach engineering was based upon a strong desire to change the face and perception of the profession. I wanted to be what I did not see in the engineering classroom as a student. I wanted to be warm, personable, attentive, approachable, different, exciting, and unique.

However, I never considered that the very need that I was trying to address would also be the source of many of my challenges. Since I am sometimes perceived as a "unicorn," a black woman in STEM with a Ph.D., I am pulled in several directions (teaching, research, mentoring, committees, speaking engagements, community service, and so on), which at times creates a dichotomy between my profession and my passion. Some say that graduate school does not teach you how to teach, but I also say that it does not prepare you to be a pioneer.

Despite these challenges, I feel that I have been relatively successful in my career. I have learned from every negative situation and used them as an opportunity to develop strategies to continue to grow while also enlightening others. Over my fifteen-year teaching career, there have been so many circumstances that highlight some aspect of being a faculty woman of color that it was difficult to select what to share. Therefore, I chose two vignettes that illustrate not only some small bias against me, but also a time where I used that opportunity to help others reframe their perception of women and underrepresented minorities as STEM professionals and educators.

Do You Need a Tutor?

One of my favorite stories happened during my first year of teaching at my new school. Many students did not realize that I had already been teaching for six years by that time. They assumed that I was new to the profession. I had a colleague who started at the same time but she had come from industry and had never taught before. Since we were teaching the same courses, I would spend a lot of time in her office helping her prepare for class.

We would typically review the day's topic and work some derivations on the whiteboard. I would provide advice on the best way to approach a topic or present it to the class. I would share notes and provide general advice on classroom management and logistics. In addition, we would sometimes go down to the classroom and work through laboratory assignments to make sure she was clear on the procedure and submission expectations.

At times during these sessions, students would come in the room to seek assistance with an assignment and we would take a break. As a prime example of how perceptions do not always match reality, that quarter I had a student write on my evaluations that "I spent many hours in my colleague's office getting 'tutored' on the course subject matter." I found that not only offensive but intriguing, since I had been teaching this very course since I was in graduate school.

I knew that there was no way that my classroom lectures gave the impression that it was new to me: therefore, there had to be something else going on. I immediately began to brainstorm ways to rectify this misconception and insure that it would never happen again. Due to this, I changed the way that I approach the first day of class.

Now I not only introduce myself on the first day of class, but also explain how many years I have been teaching, my experience with the course topic, and how I may have applied it during my years as a practicing controls engineer. I also make sure that my lectures and course organization are above reproach. As part of my mission to establish myself as a professional, I also hold my students to very exacting standards as well. In fact, my peers have actually acknowledged my work and asked me to mentor junior faculty and give new faculty teaching workshops on active learning. The good news is that I have never again been confused with a professor requiring tutoring.

Do You Need a Hug?

My next story happened very recently and is still very fresh on an emotional and intellectual level. In my institution, I have the reputation of being very professional and respectful, but also straightforward. I like to communicate clearly to my students and colleagues in order to make sure there is no confusion about my position. In other words, I am friendly and warm, but no one has ever considered me an overly affectionate individual. In fact, if you are upset, I may offer a tissue, a good talk, and maybe even a pat on the back, but never a hug. This fact is what makes the following story so fascinating.

One day, I was in a meeting with several colleagues that had become rather contentious. The primary reason was that several faculty were concerned about a new program that was proposed. There was a concern with the lack of details on implementation and connections with similar programs already in existence at the university. I also was not in support of the new program but was quiet for most of the meeting in order to learn from the feedback of others. I was one of only two women in the meeting and neither of us had spoken very much. The proponents of the program attempted to not only market the program to us but also address some of the concerns expressed. Their efforts were essentially unsuccessful in changing the minds of most individuals in the room.

After about an hour, the program's champions invited the faculty who had not spoken much to share our thoughts. I then took this opportunity to state that I would finally share my concerns with the program but would then have to leave immediately because the meeting had run long and I needed to get to another appointment.

After stating my position in what I can describe at best as in a terse yet passionate manner, I stood up to leave. I did not receive any comments on my feedback, but rather one of the presenters stood up and said, "I want to give you a hug." He then approached me and gave me a very awkward hug.

At that point, I was rendered speechless and immediately left the room with another colleague whose exiting line was, "And I don't want a hug."

It took me the evening to process how absolutely disrespectful, condescending, and patronizing that act was. I felt like my comment had been dismissed as if I was an emotional girl who was obviously overreacting and in need of unasked-for mediation. However, in order not to do just that, I thought it best to wait until the next day and process the perception of the hug with some other colleagues who were present during the meeting. The next morning when I arrived at work I had several members of my department, some of who were not even in the meeting, offer to give me a hug. It appears that good news travels fast! I knew that they were kidding but I took their offer as a prime opportunity to get feedback on the situation.

Most if not all of my colleagues agreed with my perception and encouraged me to address it. That day, I requested a meeting with the hugger. During our meeting, I first offered to clarify my position about my concerns with the program. I then went on to explain to him how I was the only African American female faculty member in the institution and that it is a constant struggle to be seen as an equal. I told him that his behavior was actually belittling. He at first did not seem to understand why I felt that way and was at a loss as to why it would be perceived as such. I then went on to ask him, "Would you have offered to hug any of the men in the room who criticized the program?" He immediately stated that he would not have and the light bulb finally came on.

I then went on to explain that not only do I not typically hug coworkers or students, but that it was also almost as if the points I made were minimized by his offer to take them away with a hug. He then stated that he had the utmost respect for me and my work and that was not his intent at all. He honestly did not have any clue that this was not the appropriate means of showing that he respected and wanted to acknowledge my position. He then apologized because he realized that it was not about his intent but rather how it was received.

My purpose was not to make him self-conscious about his behavior, but rather to make him aware of a different perspective. At the end of that meeting, I felt l that I had educated him a little about the challenges women faculty of color may face in the workplace and that offering hugs is simply not the appropriate way to address professional disagreements. We shook hands and agreed that this matter was resolved and hopefully we both went away with a much deeper understanding and mutual respect of each other.

If that were the end of this incident, that would have been great. After learning about this situation from someone else present that day, a female colleague chose to become my self-appointed advocate. No matter how much I insisted to her that I had handled and resolved the matter, she insisted on taking it to the school administration. I told her that I did not want my name involved but she used it anyway.

When she felt that the administration's response was not to her satisfaction, she then chose to broadcast what happened in a public forum and also e-mail it to all faculty on campus. She never understood that I had the right to decide how I wanted the situation addressed and that she was taking my voice away. She blatantly ignored my feelings and right to privacy. In the end, she never realized that what she did was actually worse than the original offense.

In conclusion, I don't share my stories to place blame but rather to build bridges by highlighting some of the challenges that women and faculty of color face on a daily basis. I seek to strengthen relationships and that can only come with shared experiences, mutual respect, and a strong desire to embrace diverse views. This can only be accomplished by respecting each other's feelings and destroying hidden biases.

Signed,
Patient Professor of Destiny, Purpose, and Vision

Chapter Three

Mentor Essay

Standing Firm Upon Unsteady Ground

Alford Young Jr., University of Michigan

Graduation is the best time of the academic year. I have come to this realization after six years of serving as department chair. My feeling has nothing to
do with graduation signifying reduced student traffic on campus or the refo-
cusing of faculty attention to writing, research, or vacations rather than putting business on my desk. Neither does it have to do with the arrival of the
summer (a blessed time of the year in a state like Michigan). Instead, what
makes graduation so exhilarating is that the very events comprising it allow
me to leave my desk, turn away from administrative work, and take stock of
what my service actually means to certain others.

The year 2016 involved my sixth undergraduate program reception as
department chair. In one sense, the annual event is similar. Proud parents and
family abound, as do happy graduates, faculty congratulating their (now
former) students and extending to them best wishes, and department staff
working hard to ensure that all goes well with the celebration. However, this
year's event encouraged me to pause and reflect on the meaning of being an
African American department chair.

Among this year's participating graduates was a highly regarded member
of the football team. Although the university graduation takes place in the
famed Big House, the University of Michigan football stadium, every department and program in the main undergraduate college hosts its own celebration of its graduates. Highly recognized student athletes rarely participate in
my department's event, so it was a mild surprise to see this particular one
there.

His fame notwithstanding, he behaved like every other graduate. Prior to
the start of the event he casually socialized with some of his classmates, then

took his seat when the instructions for assembling were issued, and at the appropriate time during the event he joined the line of graduates to receive accolades and a handshake from the chair as the hallmark of the celebration.

Immediately after the event's conclusion, amid parents and family taking pictures of their favorite graduate, he approached me and said, "Could I have a picture with you?" I obliged. When the picture was done I turned to him and said, "Remember what I told you in class some time ago. Your talent on the field is secondary to your talent as a student and a person." He looked at me and said thank you. He also remarked that he appreciated that I always talked to him as a regular student rather than as an athlete. He shook my hand again and then was on his way.

There was nothing especially insightful about my remarks. I said them because I vividly recalled how hard this student worked in my course. He was not remarkably talented, but he engaged with the material in ways that extended far beyond what I often experienced from other high-profile athletes in my classroom. I remember taking great pleasure in that he, an African American male, conducted himself in ways that countered the stereotypical portraits.

A few days prior to the final exam for the course he came to my office to discuss the material. He did not ask about what would be on the final exam or about what material was most important to read. Instead, he came to ensure that he understood some of its central points. At the end of our meeting, I told him what I later repeated during the photo opportunity at the graduation event: that his talent extended beyond what he demonstrated on the playing field. Since that final exam some semesters previous, I had not seen him again until the graduation event.

After the guests departed from this year's celebration, I took a seat next to one of my staff. Aside from service personnel cleaning up, we were the only people remaining in the room. I told her about how I ended up in a picture with that student (a moment that caught the attention of some people), and then about how my exchange with him caused me to reflect on the special moments I have had with parents and students over the years at the graduation ceremony.

Each year at the event's conclusion, several parents approach me to shake my hand. Most who do so are African American. Those parents in particular convey how happy they are to see someone like me holding my position. They express excitement and pride over discovering that someone who looks like them is in charge of a part of the university that was central to their children's lives. In those moments I realize that I matter to some people precisely because of who I am: an African American department chair.

I surely realize that I am a rarity. I believe I am one of three African American males to ever serve as a chair in an undergraduate college that houses nearly fifty departments and programs. About the same number of

African American women also have done so in the college. I am also the first non-Caucasian male to do so in the history of my department.

The distinctiveness of my status does not diminish the fact that, like other chairs, I have to contend with administrative challenges, sometimes-hostile faculty, and some difficult or disruptive students. Department chairs also have the constant challenge of balancing the interests and concerns of various constituencies who sometimes lack the capacity, vision, or fortitude to consider the interests of other parties as equally or more important than their own. Besides this, much of what I think about as a department chair has to do with who I am, more than with the generalities of the role.

From time to time I think about whether my racial status has much bearing on my experiences as a chair. Thinking about this is difficult because today race has lost its status as a legitimate topic for public conversation. Some may consider it a mark of progress that there has been no public discussion (or, at least none to which I have been exposed) about race as a point of concern during my service.

In the past six years I have been asked by only two department colleagues if I believed that I faced any unique challenges or difficulties in my role as a result of being African American. I responded to both that I do not believe this to be the case, but that the ways in which race has been silenced from public conversation means that I cannot really know.

What I do know is that administrators in the Dean's Office have informed me in past years that some colleagues have gone over my head with issues that should have first landed on my desk. Other colleagues have asserted that I have my own racial problems because I was investigating matters concerning allegedly inappropriate activity on their part (which, of course, I am mandated to do). Aside from these situations I can point to nothing that conjures up anything like a race effect during my term of service.

It may be a true sign of progress that my colleagues are where they are in comparison with other faculty in the academy. I also know full well that believing that I have served without having to address, react to, or defend against race is no indication that African American administrators face no such problems. In an era in which race talk in America is muted, suppressed, or avoided, it is simply hard to grasp when and how it may matter.

Ironically, there has been extensive conversation among the faculty and in the administration about the lack of a female chair in my unit's history. I have both heard about it and been invited into it. I cannot know what that may mean for the first woman to chair my unit. I must simply serve without any clear sense of what others have felt and continue to feel, positively or negatively, about me because there was no explicit conversation (at least none I was privy to) prior to my service.

For these and other reasons (the latter having to do with my having no intimate sense of what it would be like to be a chair), I approached my job with a mindset of expecting the unexpected (fully realizing that at some level this is impossible to do). I suggest that any new chair, especially one who is a first of some kind or another, should maintain that same mindset with that same realization.

Over six years I have served without having a strong sense of what others in connection to my service may do or say, or think or feel. Accordingly, being a first-ever African American chair in a department means living in liminality. Things seem to be working, as far as I know, yet there remains a strong inner feeling that I cannot know exactly what race means and how it may be made to do so in my professional life. Hence, I must try to be mindful without ever knowing what exactly to mind.

This is a hard challenge in a professional culture where almost everyone strives to be precise and exact while engaging in data analysis and other forms of research. While these principles are alive in the research lab, office, or field site, they cannot be for me—at least not in the same way—while behind the chair's desk. I urge every African American scholar who aspires to administrative service to consider how this contradiction has to be a part of one's life, and has to be so without ever being fully overcome or resolved.

A consistent lack of precise knowledge about what service may mean surely is not my only lingering thought. Indeed, I fall back on certain moments that allow me to make very specific sense of what it means to be an African American department chair. One of the best of such moments is the annual departmental graduation celebration. It is there that I feel uniquely and extraordinarily gratified. I do so because there I connect with people who do not know me and will probably never encounter me again, but who let me know quite directly that my being who I am while doing what I do is significant to them.

A true gift of the academic year is being able to absorb and relish that feeling. That moment also allows me to settle in some way with the understanding that my status as an African American chair means never knowing all that I may want to about what others around me say and feel. Embracing the positive acclaim at that moment, however fleeting it may be, is one opportunity that makes all the difference for me when I go to work behind the chair's desk. I wish that feeling upon every other African American or person of color who finds him or herself in my situation.

II

Students

Chapter Four

Research Exploring Bias in Student Ratings of Teachers

At the center of a professorship is the work of disseminating knowledge to students. Knowledge is often framed as content or discipline specific. However, the reality is that faculty often teach much more than a specific subject matter; cocurricular learning is equally important and faculty of color play a pivotal role in helping to prepare students for a diverse society. Faculty do this through formal classroom instruction, advising and mentoring, and (less directly) participation in university, community, and professional service.

Despite decades of effort, diversity in higher education has not kept up with the growing diversity of the student population. It is estimated that by 2020, minority students are expected to account for 45 percent of the country's public high school graduates, up from 38 percent in 2009 (Prescott and Bransberger, 2012). Many colleges do not reflect these changing demographics—students attending college are still predominantly white and middle class.

Graduation data reflect and show a further widening of the gap. Over the period from 1995 to 2015, the gap between white and Black 25- to 29-year-olds who had attained a bachelor's or higher degree widened from 13 to 22 percentage points, and the gap between white and Hispanic 25- to 29-year-olds at this level widened from 20 to 27 percentage points. In 2015, about 43 percent of whites between the ages of 25 and 29 had a bachelor's degree or more, compared to about 21 percent of blacks, 16 percent of Hispanics, and 63 percent of Asians (U.S. Department of Education, National Center for Education Statistics, 2016).

Faculty of color, unless teaching at a Historically Black College or University or Hispanic-Serving Institution (HSI), typically are a small minority of the faculty to which students are exposed. Students play a powerful role in

43

the lives of their professors. Research on the teaching experiences of faculty of color demonstrates that negative interactions with students inside and outside of the classroom contribute to dissatisfaction with their professorial roles and create the perception of "an uphill journey" to tenure and promotion (Harlow, 2003; Smith and Anderson, 2005).

Faculty of color often encounter a deficit of credibility from students, who undermine their authority and expertise in both subtle and not so subtle ways. Students directly challenge their credentials and intellect (Hendrix, 2007; Sampaio, 2006). Other student problematic behaviors, such as poor attitudes, disrespectful/dismissive speech, and bypassing the professor and reporting their grievances to other authorities in the university system in hopes of receiving a more favorable outcome, are daily battles. At issue, students seem to enact the question—are faculty of color "affirmative action hires"? Are they qualified to teach? Phrased more politically, the fundamental question is whether faculty of color are as effective teachers as their white peers.

Course evaluations, where students give a score for teacher effectiveness, course organization and content, the structure and "fairness" of exams, and whether they learned content, are the most common methods to evaluate teaching (Beleche, Fairris, and Marks, 2012; Clayson, 2009). These ratings influence hiring, promotions, raises, and opportunities for awards. Yet, a growing body of research suggests that a professor's race, age, accent, and even physical attractiveness could influence evaluation scores (Boring, Ottoboni, and Stark, 2016; McGowan, 2000; Subtirelu, 2015).

MacNell, Driscoll, and Hunt (2015) found that students in an online class rated the instructor's promptness in returning assignments lower when they thought their instructor was a woman (3.6 out of 5) than when they thought that instructor was a man (4.4 out of 5). Although somewhat dated, an earlier study (Tatro, 1995) found two other circumstances that can influence ratings: whether or not the class is a required course for graduation and the grade that students expect to receive. Multiple regression analysis found that both the gender of the instructor and expected grade were significant predictors of evaluation scores. Students were likely to punish women instructors more harshly with their scores when they were unhappy about required classes or disappointed with the grades they had received.

Recent studies suggest that students are more likely to comment on the appearance, clothing, and tone of voice of their women instructors in anonymous evaluations (Boring, Ottoboni, and Stark, 2016). Although much of the research on the bias embedded in the student evaluation structure focuses on gender, faculty of color experience similar biases (Harlow, 2003; Subtirelu, 2015). But the lack of research aids in dismissing their claims.

Further, the current client/customer-based model, which casts professors as suppliers who are expected to cater to students' expectations, has placed faculty of color in a uniquely disadvantaged position, as their evaluations are likely to reflect the biases of students as much as or perhaps more than the performance of the professor or the knowledge gleaned by the student.

Notably, none of these studies suggests that student ratings of professors' teaching should be eliminated or that student input is not valued. Rather, these studies suggest the importance of widening the lens through which teaching is evaluated, especially given its primacy in promotion and tenure decisions.

Often, faculty of color, queer faculty, and women are assigned to teach classes that relate to race, class, sexuality, and gender. In many cases, the professor's own background and identity becomes the object of discussion and, ironically, opens the door to charges of subjectivity, self-interest, and bias. Faculty who teach courses on such "controversial" topics are often met with resistance from students. In the classroom, they must "prove" their expertise in a topical area and do extra work to demonstrate the validity of their academic claims. Further, the incorporation of nonwhite narratives, voices of the poor, and other groups often comes as a surprise to students who have spent most of their student lives learning about white, male, and heteronormative history to the exclusion of other perspectives.

Another area of intense faculty/student interaction to receive scholarly attention is the politics of mentoring. Faculty of color have reported that they are the last approached to be advisors and mentors by students who believe that white professors are more qualified and more connected in the university system. However, although faculty of color may have fewer formal advisees, they may actually advise a large number of marginalized students on campus through informal means, like running clubs, facilitating discussion groups, or helping with career and academic planning (Griffin, 2012; Turner, Gonzalez, and Wood, 2008).

The four letters in this section underscore the complex relationships faculty of color must navigate as related to students. All four address relationships between faculty of color and students of color.

In her open letter, Sims describes a teaching moment so painful (yet so ubiquitous in the lived experiences of black women in and out of the academy) that her skill at handling the incident is nearly overshadowed. But Sims's focus is not on teacherly performance; rather it is on the well-being of her students—all her students—for, as she notes, in kindling "the fires of critical thinking and antiracism," students of color often risk being burned along with the instructor.

Mullins candidly admits her willingness to go beyond what is expected of faculty members to support students of color, and is equality candid about students of color sometimes responding negatively to this extra push. Mullins narrates an all too common experience: in the name of equity and social justice, degree candidates of color are allowed to complete programs without meeting expectations or gain approval for work that is deficient, and faculty of color are expected to agree with and wholeheartedly approve of this practice. (Mullins notes that lowering the bar happens for majority candidates, but that the consequences are much greater for candidates of color who are not only fewer in number, but also under much more scrutiny.) This benign neglect does little to advance social justice in the long run. Instead, such strategies limit the success of the one "helped" and place faculty of color in an awkward situation, within their departments, where backlash for calling out what is strikingly racist behavior is often swift.

Miller's letter picks up a battlefield theme. She writes, "I sometimes feel as if I am in fact on the front line in combat, with students, parents, administration, and faculty all aiming for me with direct fire." Miller narrates a number of instances, large and small, where her role as a teacher-scholar was criticized, challenged, downplayed, or denied. Yet the letter is one of uplift, agency, and affirmation, concluding with a message that embracing and staying true to one's authentic self is the key to thriving.

In the last letter, Ng pleads with a young black female activist to return to her class, wondering if the student did not realize that she had an ally. Narrating several jaw-dropping stories of her own encounters with racism, Ng concludes with a gentle reminder to the student-activist that "academics matter, too. . . . The stakes are too high for you to fail," and a reminder to faculty that "students need professors who are not so hidebound by adversity or cynicism that they can no longer feel the pain of others."

Mary Pattillo takes up Ng's concluding comment in her mentor essay, describing how education, accountability, and deliberative processing help her to correct any unconscious tendencies that can shape classroom interactions.

REFERENCES

Beleche, T.; Fairris, D.; and Marks, M. 2012. "Do Course Evaluations Truly Reflect Student Learning? Evidence from an Objectively Graded Post-Test." *Economics of Education Review* 31(5): 709–19.

Boring, A.; Ottoboni, K.; and Stark, P. 2016. "Student Evaluations of Teaching (Mostly) Do Not Measure Teaching Effectiveness." *ScienceOpen Research.*

Clayson, D. E. 2009. "Student Evaluations of Teaching: Are They Related to What Students Learn? A Meta-Analysis and Review of the Literature." *Journal of Marketing Education* 31(1): 16–30.

Griffin, K. 2012. "Black Professors Managing Mentorship: Implications of Applying Social Exchange Frameworks to Analyses of Student Interactions and Their Influence on Scholarly Productivity." *Teachers College Record* 114(5): 1–37.

Harlow, R. 2003. "'Race Doesn't Matter, but . . .': The Effect of Race on Professors' Experiences and Emotion Management in the Undergraduate College Classroom." *Social Psychology Quarterly* 66(4): 348–63.

Hendrix, K. G. 2007. "'She Must Be Trippin'': The Secret of Disrespect from Students of Color toward Faculty of Color." *New Directions for Teaching and Learning* (110): 85–96.

Prescott, B. T. and Bransberger, P. 2012. *Knocking at the College Door: Projections of High School Graduates*. 8th Edition. Boulder, CO: Western Interstate Commission for Higher Education.

MacNell, L., Driscoll, A., and Hunt, A. 2015. "What's in a Name: Exposing Gender Bias in Student Ratings of Teaching." *Innovative Higher Education* 40(4): 291–303.

Sampaio, A. 2006. "Women of Color Teaching Political Science: Examining the Intersections of Race, Gender, and Course Material in the Classroom." *Political Science and Politics* 39(4): 917–22.

Smith, G. and Anderson, K. J. 2005. "Students' Ratings of Professors: The Teaching Style Contingency for Latino/a Professors." *Journal of Latinos and Education* 4(2):115–36.

Subtirelu, N. 2015. "'She Does Have an Accent but . . .': Race and Language Ideology in Students' Evaluations of Mathematics Instructors on RateMyProfessors.com." *Language in Society* 44(1): 35–62.

Tatro, C. 1995. "Gender Effects on Student Evaluations of Faculty." *Journal of Research and Development in Education* 28(3): 169–73.

Turner, C., Gonzalez, J., and Wood, J. 2008. "Faculty of Color in Academe: What 20 Years of Literature Tells Us." *Journal of Diversity in Higher Education* 1(3): 139–68.

U.S. Department of Education, National Center for Education Statistics. (2016). *The Condition of Education 2016* (NCES 2016–144), *Educational Attainment of Young Adults*.

Chapter Five

Letters

LETTER 7

An Open Letter to the Black Woman in the Front Row

It was lovely having you in my class this semester. Standing in front of 200 students as the instructor of record is a daunting task for any graduate student, but it is all the more nerve wrecking when you are a black woman standing in front of 185 white students teaching a class on the sociology of race. I want to thank you for sitting in the front row. You may have noticed that I always take off my glasses just prior to beginning a lecture. I started doing this so I would not be able to see the threatening body language and hostile glares of some of your classmates. The only students I clearly see during lecture are those on the front row. Thank you for smiling at me. It meant a lot.

I know that some days you could not smile, though, and I want you to know that despite the pleasant look I've trained upon my face in the name of professionalism, I understand and share your feelings. I too was caught off guard that day a white male student countered my explanation of the low, black marriage rate as being due to structural income inequality and interpersonal, sexual racism with his own theory that blacks have low marriage rates because black women are simply "not as attractive as other women." I saw your jaw drop, I saw you look, shocked, at your friend beside you. I was glad that her face mirrored yours because, given my position, mine could not.

Though I maintained my composure and gave a measured response that beauty standards are culturally variable and it is thus only when ethnocentrically held to white aesthetics that black women are perceived as unattractive, to tell you the truth I wanted to drop decorum and just go off on that student.

49

I wanted to yell a combination of obscenities and judgments against his intelligence, not just for publicly humiliating me by suggesting, as I stood in front of 200 people, that women like me are unattractive, but for saying it while a fellow student, you, sat right in the front row minding your own business and trying to get an education.

I didn't see you smile any more that day. Instead I saw you struggle to resume taking notes as I struggled to finish the lecture. I wondered if his words were ringing in your ears as they were in mine. I wondered if you too felt that the eyes of everyone in the room were now upon you, looking at every part of your body and evaluating it to decide whether his words applied to you or whether you were the exception—that is, "pretty for a black girl." I saw you leave, walking quickly and speaking to no one, as soon as I dismissed class.

I wanted to run after you, but I didn't. I watched you go because what I would have said would have just made you feel worse: Welcome to academia. Welcome to a place where black women are first presumed incompetent and then, when that initial assumption has been irrefutably disproven, are dismissed ad hominem. I didn't run after you because I would have also had to say that this is just your freshman year: Get ready, it gets worse. Last semester, for example, a white male student suggested, given the statistics that children born to single mothers are at higher risk of poverty, that black women should "just stop having kids."

I did not want to yell that day; I wanted to leave the room right that second and go hug my goddaughter. I wanted to cry my eyes out that we live in a world where people think children like her should not exist. I wanted to cry, too, in frustration that for all my charts, statistics, and painstakingly worded and memorized lecture scripts, I still hadn't been able to get through to some students the basic sociological fact that social problems—including and especially problems of racial and economic inequality—are caused more by unequal social arrangements than by completely individual malpractices and poor choices.

Had I run after you that day I fear I would have had nothing comforting to say, so instead I went to my office and wrote you that e-mail acknowledging the comment and extending an invitation to come to office hours if you needed to talk. I was glad that you replied, but I must admit that your e-mail made me feel worse. It made me feel worse when you confirmed my fears that the comment had interrupted your ability to concentrate for the rest of the class period and the rest of the day. It made me feel worse when you said you knew that I, as the professor could not "attack" the student and so you were upset at yourself for not standing up to him. The university should be a place of learning and exploring, yet for us, no matter where we are in the classroom, it is a place in which we have to fight and protect each other.

I'm sorry I could not protect you from such hurtful ignorance. I'm glad, though, that the TAs were able to use the incident as a catalyst for a larger discussion of the social construction of cultural standards the next week. I hope you saw in your small group discussion what I saw in additional e-mails I received later that day: that we were not the only ones who were offended. White students messaged me that they too thought the comment was "disgusting and offensive." One white woman said that she turned around and glared at the student who said it.

The other students who wrote me also told me how impressed they were with how well I handled the situation. Students often tell me how well I deal with difficult topics, and every year I receive at least one e-mail from a former student testifying that because of my class and others like it s/he now views the world through a more critical lens. And while these comments are honestly what makes teaching difficult topics meaningful and worthwhile to me, I know that white students' having epiphanies years later is little comfort in the moment to those of you who get burned with me as I kindle the fires of critical thinking and antiracism.

It was unfair to you emotionally and academically to have to experience that student's comment, and it is unfair that more things like it are going to happen to you again. My unsolicited advice is to take those comments, take others' assumptions of your unworthiness, look them in the eye and resoundingly reject them. See them as the desperate, last-ditch attempt of white patriarchy to keep us in our "place" and *reject them*. I hope my smile to you the next days after that comment let you know that your "place" is right there in the lecture hall seat, the same as everyone else's; and I want you to know that your smile was a daily reminder to me that my place is right there in the front of the room.

Congratulations on completing your first year in college,
and best wishes for the future,
JPS

LETTER 8

Dear Black and Racialized Students,

In many of our backgrounds we are storytellers, so I am going to tell you a story. You may not like it but it is my truth, and I am telling my story as I see it and as it unfolds in my life as a black woman teacher. My story is about the relationship, that you and I have in the academy: but to be clear, I am going to give you a general description about my experience of how you, white students, and my colleagues see me, and then I will remind you of a painful incident that happened among us. Prior to sharing my story with you, I want you to know how I feel about you.

When I see you in the hallways, in one of my classes, in a crowded room on campus or at a conference, my heart fills with joy as I know that another one of us has entered the race. My wish is always to see you sprint across the finish line like Usain Bolt, the Jamaican track and field superstar and the fastest man on earth. Sometimes when we initially meet, you are joyous, too, and I can see the relief in your eyes and on your body that someone wants to hear your story, since you are not the ones the masses gather around.

They only gather around you if you have a certain *type* of story to tell, the one that includes retelling your experience of carnage. To me, you are a person with aspirations, pain, and goals, and your experiences of carnage do not define who you are. In those moments when you are ignored, we speak the same language and you appreciate my company, if only fleetingly.

When you begin to search for or solidify your place in the academy, our one moment passes quickly. You get caught up in the stereotypes of who others tell you that I am and for your own survival and success, we become oil and water. If you protected yourself and carried on, that would be one thing, but you buy into the stories that are handed down to you by power holders in the ivory towers; you allow those stories to define my being, crawl under your skin, settle into your pores, drain into your blood, and poison your body—and that makes it easy for you to believe that I am a replica of the harpy.

In her article "Who You Callin' Nappy Headed?" (2009), Ladson-Billings chronicles my experience with you and many others, including white students and colleagues. Before we actually meet, you have conjured up a caricature of a beastly, wretched, and wicked black woman teacher. You forget that your socialized antiblack knowledge of me is a reflection of you as a black or racialized person.

Antiblack racism shapes the discourse of my position as a black woman teacher who is said to have "high expectations," which results in certain failure for students; I am "a hard marker," which means that I "don't give As"; my toughness drives students to tears; and my unapproachability invokes fear among students, staff, and faculty (Course Evaluations 2004–2015; Personal Communication).

My evaluative comments are derived from mostly white students. The question is, am I tougher on you than on them? I have a soft spot for you, but no, I am not harder on you. Simply put, I have built my career on academic integrity, scholarly rigor, and transparency. I admit that sometimes I am more supportive of you than I am of white students.

I admit that sometimes I am more supportive of you than I am of white students, but this does not mean that I am unsupportive of white students. I know from experience that they need me less, as they have more choices than you do with white professors who are ready and willing to support them. You do not have the type of mentorship that provides you with advanced-level experience, such as graduate supervision, team funding application, publishing, and research mentorship.

Naturally, my own experiences shape my commitment to your success, so I happily morph into the supportive mentor encouraging, sharing, and most importantly acknowledging your experiences of racism in academe. Since I know intimately many of the experiences you detail about racism, misogyny, and microaggressions, it is easy for me to help refocus you on your strengths and encourage you to visualize success.

However, I realize that a few of you, whom I am eager to mentor unconditionally, have issues not necessarily related to institutional barriers. For example, you submit unprofessional and incomplete work, frequently blame others for your academic challenges, become upset with critical feedback, refuse to engage in open conversation about your work or take responsibility for your own learning. Instead, you tell me "this is what white teachers do" when I challenge your work.

In one case, I reviewed your dissertation and was embarrassed for you that your supervisory committee, which was comprised of both black and white faculty members, allowed your work to proceed to the review level. I assessed your dissertation as not being ready for a defense. However, my recommendations motivated an onslaught of e-mails and telephone calls from individuals attached to you. I received fifteen e-mails, numerous text messages, eleven telephone calls, and I spent almost nine hours on the telephone with you and your committee, defending, rationalizing, and justifying my recommendations.

You and your committee members used the same racist institutional tools that others use to question my competence and discredit my recommendations. Confidential information about my recommendation was exposed and others suggested that I had sabotaged your defense. I was accused of grandstanding, being tough on you because we are both black, and having too high expectations. I was questioned about my understanding of a Ph.D. defense and my role as a reviewer in the dissertation process while, simultaneously, members of your committee remarked that you are "not sharp."

I was urged to recant my recommendation to allow you to proceed to your defense with a promise that my concerns would be attended to in a follow-up process. I was led to believe that you had suffered severe emotional consequences as a result of my recommendations. I braced myself for the backlash of rejecting the status quo; but I also hung my head in shame for not being able to push you further. I waited for the stories about me to float around and motivate my isolation.

The conflict made me feel uncomfortable; I was sick for seven days; I could not sleep, concentrate, or eat. My conscience bothered me; I felt guilty for seemingly colluding with racist institutional policies that I know disadvantaged you throughout your Ph.D. program, and I blamed myself for the stress that you were experiencing.

The most challenging part of the experience was the pressure to assign you a pass, in spite of the deficiencies in your dissertation. I was committed to supporting you in improving your work to an acceptable academic standard, but you and your committee only wanted to use me as a rubber stamp. You had no interest in doing the work and honoring the participants in your research. "Just tell me what to do," you told me, and "I just want to finish."

There is an institutional code of conduct that seems to suggest that racialized and black students, especially those at the graduate level, must pass their coursework and successfully defend their thesis and dissertations regardless of the state of your final product. This idea of trying to level the playing field is complex given the persistence of racism and marginalization that you experience in academe. I understand why faculty and administrators may want to award you a pass when your work does not meet basic standards for your academic levels. However, I refuse to acquiesce to a lack of academic integrity.

My race politics are clearly demonstrated in my research and teaching scholarship. I will support you unconditionally as long as you are willing to try your best and put the work in to produce academic products of a reasonable quality; however, you need to take responsibility for your own learning and seek support when you need to. I realize that this may be an unpopular position, especially since white students are regularly promoted when they, too, are not qualified.

I recently recommended that a white student was not ready for the Ph.D. defense, but she was pushed through without objections or critique from anyone else. Nonetheless, I believe that awarding you a fraudulent pass is a blight on academic integrity among scholars like us. Many of you are academically capable; I recently reviewed a Ph.D. dissertation and a Master's thesis, both of which were outstanding. Therefore, I remain hopeful and committed to maintaining the highest level of integrity and rigor in my own work and my dealings with all students—regardless of race.

Sincerely,
Delores Mullings

LETTER 9

Dear Fellow Front-of-the-Room Academicians,

I teach and advise undergraduates. I chair a department that houses two degree programs and thirteen faculty members. I sit on academic committees as well as community and professional boards. I am tenured and have been at my university—an HBCU—longer than I initially planned, for about thirteen years. I am at the Front of the Room!

I sometimes feel as if I am at the Front of the Room while simultaneously sitting in the back corner of that same room, given the various challenges, tasks, and experiences I have faced over this more-than-decade. With the multiple hats I wear, I sometimes feel as if I am in fact on the front line in combat, with students, parents, administration, and faculty all aiming for me with direct fire. Yet, I am still standing and sitting in the Front of the Room. How? I relate to the old spiritual: "My soul looks back and wonders how I got over?"

As I look back, my story begins with my excitement to have the opportunity to teach at a historically black university. All of my prior experience had been at majority white institutions—small, private, public, and large—and I was thrilled to teach at an institution where I thought race and ethnicity would no longer be a defining restriction.

I was wrong.

When I first came to my institution, I was in black culture euphoria—for about one week. Once classes began, and I began to engage with the students, I was quickly told by some faculty and students that I emphasized my blackness too much. That this is already an HBCU; I didn't have to talk about race, ethnicity, or black history. I was told that I should focus on being more global, which in this case meant less black. I didn't know what to do.

I found myself questioning my own blackness as a result of this initial backlash. I was teaching an introductory course for our majors that focused on the development of students' critical thinking capacity following Bloom's taxonomy—cognitive levels of comprehension, understanding, synthesis, and evaluation. It seemed like a natural fit for me to pull current events as discussion topics that spoke to the students' experiences as persons of color in a world that even fifteen years ago—and sadly, still today—often treated them as second-class citizens.

Today, I can't recall the exact issue that I pulled for that particular discussion, but I know I looked at politics and race relations. One student—and this I do recall quite specifically—asked me, "Dr. Miller, why are you so black?" I remember standing in the front of the classroom, tilting my head to the left looking puzzled. I retorted, "What do you mean? I *am* black." She said, "Everything we do in this class is about black people and black experiences and black lives. . . . I thought this class was about critical thinking." While she was speaking, I glanced at the rest of the class and saw heads nodding and eyes glossing over in agreement. I was shocked!

Here I was teaching at an HBCU in the South, excited to work toward positively impacting and empowering black students by providing them with contextually relevant research, data, and tools centered on their blackness, and they didn't want it! What was I to do? I didn't really answer her question. . . . I remember stating something about the fact that being black is who I am: I can't turn it off and on. It makes me, me. She nodded, and we went on with the class, but I was disturbed.

After the class, I mentioned this to one of my colleagues who had been at the university for at least a decade already. He, an African male, shared with me that the African American students don't want to learn about Africa or African American history: they want to fit in. I questioned his response, but did take heed.

Fast-forward a couple of years. I was in a university curriculum committee meeting proposing a program and additional required courses that focus on African and African American culture and history as part of the general education core. I was told by the then–Vice President of Academic Affairs that we don't need to offer such courses because we are a black school. But what makes us a black school, I wondered—merely having a majority of black students?

I thought that what made us a black school was that we provided a particular educational approach that is culturally sensitive and relevant to the students we teach in response to centuries of racist educational systems. For me, to teach at an HBCU meant that I could take on a social, cultural, and political responsibility to empower and uplift. Fortunately, there were other faculty members who agreed, and today, we still require all students to take six credit hours (the equivalent of two three-credit courses) in cultural electives.

Even with the cultural elective requirement, I was still "too black." So I embraced it; I chair the university's Black History Month programming and the Dr. Martin Luther King Jr. Commemoration programs. I am among the university's qualified "go to" spokespersons on issues regarding black women and culture.

As I continue to fast-forward, I realize that today, I just may have an answer for my student, who has graduated and is successful as a result of attending an HBCU. I am "so black" because that is all I know to be—it is simply who I am. I am "so black" because it has helped me to survive. I call on my black faith and my black ethos to help me survive. I recall, remember, and rely on the strategies of my foremothers and forefathers—strategies of resistance, hope, perseverance, and prayer. I remember the sacrifices of my grandmother, great aunt, and other family members who cleaned the homes of white folks, picked cotton, and toiled land with their bare hands, so that my siblings and I could attend colleges.

My blackness is my ability to survive and thrive. My blackness is my pride. My blackness is my safety net. It is my comfort zone as well as who and what I am. My blackness provides a safe space and place to reflect, read, research, write, and cope. My blackness is what allows me to "get real" with students, faculty and parents. My blackness is an authentic attribute that can be recognized by others who are "so black!"

So, at the Front of the Room, I bring my blackness with me. I encourage you, my younger brothers and sisters in the academy, regardless of your institution's alignment, to embrace who you are. Embrace all of you and do not be ashamed. Feminist scholar bell hooks writes, "Each time a woman begins to speak, a liberating process begins." I propose to take this even further: each time a *person of color* speaks, liberation occurs. For we are creating a space where often there is none or very little space—we are pushing ourselves toward the margins and moving toward the center. In being your true, authentic, ethnic self, you are not biased or hegemonic. Instead, you are free.

Sometimes though, in the midst of that liberating space, you find that there are other ways that you can be marginalized when at the Front of the Room. One such instance is in the simple, yet profound, aspect of naming and titles. I have a colleague who recently earned his terminal degree. However, when he first came to the university, he was still in graduate school. This white scholar would be called "Dr." without hesitation. However, yours truly would be called "Ms." or "Mrs.," although my door signs, syllabus, and contact information throughout campus all indicate that I hold a Ph.D.

Example number two: An African American man who is older than I was a professional staff member, and a colleague of mine. This staff member did not hold any terminal degrees. Yet, students would often refer to him as "Dr." instead of "Mr.", while still refusing to call me "Dr." or even "Professor"—even when alerted to my academic status as a faculty member. Initially, I said, "Well it is no big deal," but then I realized that their refusal to acknowledge my academic credentials speaks to something larger than them, or even than myself. It speaks to a system that downplays the academic achievements of not only women, but specifically women of color.

This was further reiterated when we hired a new faculty member who was not African American, but Filipina. She was considerably younger than most of the faculty, and students initially called her "Ms." However, quickly (with some advice from yours truly to set a formal bar with her students), they called her "Dr." Yet, we find that our older male colleagues rarely refer to her as "Dr.", but by her first name. This is not merely when in a casual setting, but often in formal instances, and sometimes even when amongst students.

Lastly, I asked some sistah-colleagues (other women of color faculty members) and they, too, could easily recall multiple instances of being pushed to a "Mrs." or "Ms." title, rather than being addressed as "Professor" or "Dr." We all experienced this from other colleagues, as well as from students and parents.

Even more recently, I was given the opportunity to check myself. An African American colleague of mine recently earned her doctorate. By habit, I would often refer to her as "Ms." But with the terminal degree, I had to make a concerted effort to call her "Dr." to show her the respect that she deserves. I don't want to downplay her accomplishments, or perpetuate a slight toward another female faculty of color.

My point is not to be petty. Rather, my point is to share instances that may on the surface seem insignificant, but may also hold deeper meaning with lasting negative impact. Who you are, what you are called, and how people see you impacts your relationship with them, and to a certain extent, impacts the level of your effectiveness as a member of academia. I encourage you, my brothers and sisters, to be *you*. Embrace your ethnicity, culture, race, ethos, and spirit. Find ways to maintain composure in the Front of the Room; yet, do not compromise your integrity or dismiss your beliefs.

For me, the Front of the Room is a space that takes a special breed of person—one who is committed, strong, reliable, responsible, accountable, fluid, and flexible—and knows her/himself. I have survived both microaggressions and larger incidents, as a result of being a black woman in higher education; yet, I still stand because of the very identifier that holds a historical, spiritual, and social significance—my blackness. I am "so black" and I am at the Front of the Room, standing tall.

Signed,
I'm Black and I'm Proud

LETTER 10

In Solidarity, Dear Student,
I have been meaning to write to you for some time, ever since you stopped coming to class. I know that you have been busy mobilizing support for the black female students involved in the "bus incident" who are now facing criminal charges. I reach out to you in solidarity.

You gave an impassioned speech at the campus rally the other day. You invoked Audre Lorde, and it was clear that you took to heart and translated into action her essays "The Uses of Anger: Women Responding to Racism" and "The Transformation of Silence into Language and Action." These essays, from her book *Sister Outsider*, are required readings in many of the courses offered by our department. I was so proud of you that evening.

I reach out to you in solidarity—but would you accept it? I am uncertain because although you have stopped coming to my class you did not do the same in your other graduate seminar, taught by a black female professor. I am not a stranger to you because I was your academic advisor during the entire time you were an undergraduate major in our department. We were able to talk openly and freely about racism, sexism, classism, and intersectionality. But clearly something has changed, because we are not having these conversations anymore. Is it because I am Asian? Perhaps in the context of the "Black Lives Matter" struggle, you no longer trust me to be an ally? Or, at the very least, you don't think that I would understand your pain?

Asians in America are both visible and invisible. We are visible in the sense that we are always already viewed as "alien." Let me share one incident that happened many years ago when I was visiting my niece in Portland, Oregon.

She was four years old at the time. I took her to a neighborhood playground with a sandbox because she loved building sand castles. As she was patting down a castle wall a boy came up to her and asked, "Did you miss your plane?" Even as I was processing the question, my niece answered, "I was born here!" I felt like someone had kicked me in the gut. For a four-year-old girl to answer what seemed to be an innocent question the way she did (and so promptly, too) suggested that she had been taunted before for being "foreign" and told that she should "go back where you came from."

A few years later, when she was in first grade, she began having stomach pains that puzzled her parents and pediatrician. Why would a seven-year-old show symptoms of ulcers? The eureka moment was when she confided in me about a birthday party at her classmate's home. There were the usual balloons and games and general merriment, but whereas the other children were left to play, her classmate's mother asked my niece to help in the kitchen. "Who did she think I am, her maid?" She belonged in the party only as a (foreign) domestic servant.

I told my niece that it was okay to be angry. Indeed, she should be angry. We should *all* be more visibly angry. The sight of an angry Asian woman can be a shock to the system. Mitsuye Yamada, in her essay "Invisibility Is an Unnatural Disaster: Reflections of an Asian American Woman" (in Moraga and Anzaldua, 1983, 35–40), recounts a heated class discussion of the introduction to *Aiiieeeee!*, an anthology of works by Asian American writers. It turned out that her students were offended by the anger of Asian Americans: "It made me angry. *Their* anger made *me* angry, because I didn't even know the Asian Americans felt oppressed. I didn't expect their anger."

The invisibility of oppression suffered by Asian Americans means that our pain is not understood. "Why are you so angry?" It also means that our work in anti-oppression coalitions are all too often invisible and our contributions overlooked. This is true in academic settings, too. Once, I was a faculty facilitator for a curriculum development workshop organized by the Association for American Colleges and Universities. After two days of intense work on how to design courses that incorporate "diversity," participants gave their feedback in the town hall session. One of them, who actually was in my section, complained, "The faculty lacks diversity! I don't see any faculty of color!" It was a valid complaint—the lack of diversity—but did she see me at all, her facilitator for the past two days? *Who does she think I am, the maid?*

Did I tell you about my experience at my previous employer, a flagship university in the south-central U.S.? Shortly after I began my tenure-track job there, a colleague shared with me that after I was offered the job, a member of the faculty said, "Good, now we have a Chinese cook!" The association of me with food extended even to students.

At the end of the first semester, one student wrote in the teaching evaluation, "All I learned in this course is not to order egg rolls in a Chinese restaurant!" Other students missed that nugget of wisdom because my accent was too thick for them to comprehend. I stopped reading these evaluations for many years. In time, I earned the respect and affection of my students, but I continued to be alienated from my colleagues. Nonetheless, despite the lack of mentoring from senior colleagues, I earned tenure and promotion and eventually was elected president of my professional association. When the position of chair of my present department was advertised, I went for it.

When I started this letter I had no intention of including a litany of my encounters with racism. I am sharing these stories with you in solidarity, to let you know that you can count on me to understand and to be your ally. These are stories of survival. I want you to know that, for me, these adversities have only made me stronger. They motivate me to be the kind of person that I am. I practice the Chinese golden rule: "Do not do unto others what you do not want others to do unto you." I am also guided by Audre Lorde who, in "The Uses of Anger," cautioned me not to be too self-referential, "What woman here is so enamored of her own oppression that she cannot see her heel print upon another woman's face? What woman's terms of oppression have become so precious and necessary to her as a ticket into the fold of the righteous, away from the cold winds of self-scrutiny?" (Lorde, 1984, 132).

However, I am first and foremost your professor. It is my duty to remind you that academics matter, too. You wrote in your application for admission to our graduate program the reason why you wanted to pursue an advanced degree. You wanted to work in the higher education field, in order to create a more equitable world for all. If this is still your goal, please: do not cut any more classes. The stakes are too high for you to fail. Academia needs more people like you. Students need professors who are not so hidebound by adversity or cynicism that they can no longer feel the pain of others.

Sincerely,
Vivien Ng

REFERENCES

Lorde, A. 1984. *Sister Outsider: Essays and Speeches by Audre Lorde*. Berkeley, CA: Crossing Press.

Moraga, C. and Anzaldua, G. (eds.). 1983. *This Bridge Called My Back: Writings by Radical Women of Color*. New York: Kitchen Table Press.

Chapter Six

Mentor Essay

Don't Forget to Reflect On and Fight Your Own Biases

Mary Pattillo, Northwestern University

One of the hardest things I've faced as a teacher dealing with students is balancing a disposition of authority with a disposition of humility. Authority and humility are not opposites. Our students will not accept what we say if we don't convey a recognition that we are not gods, but merely humans who have read a lot of books. So, authority and humility are two necessary traits that we attempt to hold in productive balance. They align nicely with other important dispositional pairs. For example, a teacher always allows herself to also be a learner; and a professor—while required to "profess" for most of the class—should also be quiet sometimes and reflect. If you are not also a listener (and a reader), you risk spouting irrelevant, outdated, and even offensive information, passing it off as knowledge.

It is in this spirit of cultivating humility and reflection that I share this confession with you. I am a black woman academic who has repeatedly and badly "flunked" tests of implicit racial and gender bias. Perhaps you've heard of these tests, mostly run out of Harvard University's Project Implicit. They are widely discussed in the popular media, and they are supported by hundreds of academic studies that confirm their validity and usefulness for studying what goes in our heads without our even knowing it. Indeed, they seem to measure things in our heads that might even be contrary to what we profess out loud.

The Implicit Association Test (IAT) measures the speed with which we make associations between faces and words, or pairs of words. How fast and accurately do you connect black faces with positive words like "happiness"? How easy is it for you to connect female names with leadership qualities? The variations of the test are vast, covering religion, sexuality, skin tone, gender in science, body size, and many more. And I've flunked more than one.

I'm a sociologist who studies and teaches about inequalities, so taking the IAT definitely wasn't the first time I thought about the likelihood that I had internalized racial and gender bias. That consciousness has been there since my early days as a professor. I've always had a good representation of men of color and women of all races in my classes and among my advisees. And I often fretted that I was alternately favoring or undervaluing them.

Have you ever wondered that, too? Am I grading Latino students more harshly? Am I calling on women more? Am I smiling more at black students? Am I letting (white) men dominate the conversation? Am I giving more (or less) verbal encouragement to white women, Latino men, black cismen, white transgendered students, dark-skinned men, Asian lesbians, etcetera, etcetera? The opportunities for wrongdoing are enough to paralyze you. And, yet, you have to stand up and teach, with authority.

I imagine that students of color and women feel a sense of safety in my classroom and in my presence. But I've learned that being a black woman doesn't just magically create a welcoming and fair space for all students. I can't just point my finger innocently at my white male colleagues as the containers of all things racist. To really be humble, I have to reflect on my own biases and work to eradicate them in my interactions with students.

But "black people can't be racist," you protest. I know racism isn't about bad individuals with racist thoughts, but instead about systems, structures, and institutions. I am a product of these forces just as everybody else is. So are you. And, let's be real, we are now (semi-) privileged members of those systems by dint of our educational and occupational status. Our systemic understanding of these forces should make us hyperaware that we can be guilty of perpetuating racism simply by enacting a business-as-usual attitude. Without actively working to disrupt the systems that oppress us, we reproduce them.

But who am I to get all preachy? I apparently have deep and deeply bad thoughts about black people and women. I was definitely surprised by my results on the IAT. I grew up and have mostly lived in black neighborhoods, went to a black elementary school, attended a black church, have a family full of black people, listen to black music, read black books, and love a black man (pardon the heteronormativity). Even my dog growing up was black! I am not lacking in positive black imagery. And the same goes for my exposure to wonderful, smart, and powerful women. But I guess none of that can fully combat the many messages of white superiority. Sure, I belted out beautiful black gospel music in church, but at the end of the day we were singing to a white Jesus.

I am, of course, not alone in internalizing racism. Project Implicit (2016) reports that "approximately even numbers of Black respondents show[ing] a pro-White bias as show[ing] a pro-Black bias." I'm even a more typical woman, since women are more likely than men to associate careers with men and families with women (Nosek et al., 2007). Still, it's no consolation to be among friends on the *wrong* side of the issue.

So, what do I do with my explicit knowledge of my implicit bias? What should *you* do? The psychology literature gives us some anti-biasing strategies. I use a few of them, namely education, accountability, and deliberative processing.

First, I read up on implicit bias. I'm comforted to know that it cannot, by any means, be 100 percent predictive of behavior, and my countervailing explicit antiracist attitudes likely push me closer to fairness in how I treat my students.

Second, I try to keep myself accountable; that is, I always assume that I will have to justify my grading, my divvying out of approving nods, and my critical feedback. And I assume that my judges are students of color and women who write my course evaluations and talk to their friends about me. By assuming that they are watching me or may ask me for an explanation, I hope to correct whatever unconscious tendencies I have to expect less of them or treat them badly. Maybe I overcorrect at times. (If you let white [male] students tell it, any second taken away from attention on *them* is an overcorrection.) But I figure that some extra positive reinforcement is hardly reparations for the depth of my and others' bias.

Finally, deliberative processing is related to accountability and education since you first must be educated about the problem in order to think through it. Then you must have some motivation (i.e., a sense of accountability) to *slow down and examine* what you're doing as you profess, teach, and wield authority.

These are all very much individual fixes; activities I do to try to correct the prejudices inside my head. They don't, however, reflect my training as a sociologist. So I also try to change some structural things in my classroom. I often grade "blind" by having students put their student identification numbers on their papers rather than their names. This blind assessment strategy has worked to get more women into symphony orchestras, for example (Goldin and Rouse, 2000).

I also make sure my syllabi include plenty of entries by scholars of color and women, and I show media clips that positively portray black and brown people. More and more, I'm trying to teach about resistance, creativity, and intelligence in black and other marginalized communities. When you teach about racial inequality, the data are unrelenting in their portrait of black unemployment, Hispanic school failure, and women's lower earnings. So I work to balance these "downer" images with counter-stereotypic examples. My hope is that these practices inoculate the whole classroom from the unconscious bias I have not cured in myself and that surely also resides in some of them.

A key component of Patricia Hill Collins's (1989) black feminist ways of knowing and learning is an ethic of caring. I deploy an ethic of caring in my classroom in order to combat the stew of implicit and explicit racism and sexism (and homophobia and classism) that permeates our society and universities, and that dwells within us. I have to care enough about the black and brown and women students in my charge, which ultimately means caring enough about myself, to be vigilant against using my bias-soaked authority to their detriment. Instead, I humbly recognize that I am on my journey, still far from having arrived.

REFERENCES

Collins, Patricia Hill. 1989. "The Social Construction of Black Feminist Thought." *Signs* 14(4): 745–73.

Goldin, Claudia and Cecilia Rouse. 2000. "Orchestrating Impartiality: The Impact of 'Blind' Auditions on Female Musicians." *American Economic Review* 90(4): 715–41.

Nosek, Brian A.; Smyth, Frederick L.; Hansen, Jeffrey J.; Devos, Thierry; Lindner, Nicole M.; Ranganath, Kate A.; Smith, Colin Tucker; Olson, Kristina R.; Chugh, Dolly; Greenwald, Anthony G.; and Banaji, Mahzarin R. 2007. "Pervasiveness and Correlates of Implicit Attitudes and Stereotypes." *European Review of Social Psychology* 18(1): 36–88.

Project Implicit. 2016. "FAQs." https://implicit.harvard.edu/implicit/demo/background/faqs.html#faq19. Accessed March 5, 2016.

III

Tenure

Chapter Seven

Literature on Teaching, Research, and Service

Studies show that many nonwhite faculty view the tenure process as obscure and fraught with contradictions (Rice, Sorcinelli, and Austin, 2000; O'Merara, 2002) and basically flawed (Edwards, 1999; Gappa and Trice, 2009). On the way to tenure, they relate that they experienced feelings of isolation, alienation, exploitation, and imposter syndrome that resulted from their perception that some of their white colleagues presumed that they were less qualified than white academics to do the job for which they were hired (Ek et al., 2010; Flores and Garcia, 2009; Harris and Gonzales 2012; Turner, 2002).

To borrow from an organizational socialization perspective (Bauer et al., 2007), the tenure process can be seen as a mechanism of transforming "outsiders" (newly hired faculty) to "insiders" (tenured faculty) within the academy. The transition takes place over a period of six or so years, and during that time, new initiates must learn and adjust—or are socialized—to their role and the culture of the institution, learn about how to fulfill the duties they are assigned, and finally, meet or exceed the assessment criteria for gaining the prize—that is, tenure.

Therefore, tenure is also a "test"—if you will—that outsiders must pass. Most colleges and universities claim to have a fair, transparent, and objective tenure and promotion evaluation process that simply assesses one's research, teaching, and service (weighed differently in different universities). While most universities have documents that have general descriptions of the promotion and tenure (P&T) process, including things like the kinds of achievements that are recognized and the role of the P&T committee, we know of no institution that clearly and overtly outlines exactly how many publications in which journals, what average score on teaching evaluations, or how many hours of committee work during a five-year period will be sufficient to garner tenure. And since policy or documentation regarding these important details is seldom available, bias seems almost essential to the tenure and promotion process (Jones et al., 2014).

In an ethnographic study of the tenure and promotion process in several STEM departments at a major university, Jones and his colleagues (2014) report that, regardless of the documents created to guide junior faculty through the P&T process, those who were in a bid for this advancement reported that many unwritten guidelines existed, and that these, ultimately, were more important than the ones that were put to paper. To follow the assessment metaphor, if tenure is a test, then few, if any, of the individual test questions are objective.

Speaking about tenure as a prize at the end of a test period also suggests an oversimplification of the process and may obscure the ways in which achieving excellence in the faculty trifecta—teaching, scholarship, and service—may be more difficult for people of color than their white counterparts. Research suggests that faculty of color are more likely than other faculty to use a wider range of teaching strategies like active learning strategies, and though these may increase student learning outcomes, they represent a divergence from the norm for students and lower teaching evaluations often reflect their classes' discomfort (Cole and Barber, 2003; Umbach, 2006).

In terms of research and scholarly output, the literature shows that that which is produced by faculty of color is often viewed by their faculty peers as less rigorous, niche—meaning more likely to be about "minority" populations and therefore not mainstream—and trivial (Stanley, 2006; Joseph and Hirshfield, 2010). Too, because research that is more likely to address issues of interest, or pertaining, to people of color is less likely to find its way into top-tier disciplinary journals, in this age of impact factors, citation matrices, and unquestioned devotion to leading journals and academic presses, faculty of color are truly at a disadvantage (Harley et al., 2010). How so?

Though never explicitly stated, it is often "known" within an institution that faculty research is valued differently in terms of the type of knowledge being produced, where it is published, if it garners grants and other awards, and how much prestige it may bring to the university; scholarship pertaining to non-majority concerns and published in so-called "second-tier" journals by researchers perceived to be less important is therefore likely to be a less than ideal fit for most universities.

Service, the last of the three areas of assessment for P&T, is also fraught for faculty of color. Most academics would agree that of the three areas of assessment, less weight is put on service than on the other two. Service can be thought of as the "good citizen" test and it is assessed in a number of ways. These include serving on committees (both at the departmental and university-wide levels), mentoring and advising students (formally and informally), working on activities that promote or serve one's discipline (activities such as planning symposia, serving on disciplinary association committees at the national level), and even "representing" the university to alums, donors, and parents.

So while service may not be viewed with the gravitas of scholarship and teaching, faculty of color often relate that they experience feelings of stress associated with some service obligation. Racial/ethnic identity and visible identities are often reasons why faculty of color are asked to serve on many committees and, especially in the case of "diversity"-related committees, they are overburdened with these tasks in predominantly white institutions (Gardner, 2013; Misra et al., 2011). Universities, according to Kelly and McCann (2014), can cause nonwhite faculty to feel as if they are being utilized (both in terms of their physical presence and their skills) to meet structural diversity goals, even as they are made to feel "othered" and devalued within their departments and campuses.

Colleges and universities throughout the United States are admitting more and more nonwhite students. They must also respond to the larger social factors at play in contemporary society. Within the past two years, we have witnessed the eruption of a number of race-related schisms in our society—from the shooting of unarmed black men, women, and boys in communities large and small across the nation, to the harassment and discontent of black student and faculty on university campuses. These situations place burdens on institutions of higher learning to respond to, if not lead, the charge of dealing with the ravages of racial discrimination. The presence of faculty of color on campuses is often a response that institutions can visibly display as proof that they are invested in issues of diversity and social justice.

So even as universities frame decisions about promotion and tenure as being objectively evaluated, faculty of color often report that based on their experience, the process is anything but impartial. Instead of being transparent and clear, the evaluation process was seldom explicitly revealed. Objectivity, in terms of evaluation, was almost impossible; committees of evaluators, of course, bring their own inter-subjectivity, thereby rendering the assumption that the 'worth' of a candidate's scholarship, teaching or even service will find universal favor inherently flawed (Baez, 2003; Urrietta et al., 2015). Different members of a committee can interpret one tenure file differently. When such a situation occurs, whose interpretation of the file is going to prevail? Faculty who serve on P&T committees report how tenure expectations are applied differently to different candidates and how subjective characteristics (such as if a candidate is well-liked or considered a "good fit" for the institution) are subtly or overtly discussed and considered during tenure cases (Urrieta et al., 2015).

The letters in this section mirror the twists and turns of the road to tenure. Ghaffar-Kucher's letter challenges us to consider how the idea of tenure pits those who own or are on the path toward the coveted status are pitted against those academics—so-called "contingent" or adjunct faculty—who teach in institutions of higher education without the protections that tenure offers. She contends that both groups' labor may be exploited, and at great personal (emotional, physical, and spiritual) cost.

Santos's letter to his mentors draws our attention to the tremendous labor that faculty of color perform in the name of furthering an institution's "diversity." He, too, poignantly describes the cost associated with not only addressing the inequities that nonwhite faculty, students, and staff encounter in the academy, but also how this work can get in the way of scholarly production—that which we are told is the most important element for earning tenure and promotion. Santos readily admits that, as a Latino who was pulled into "diversity work," his scholarship suffered and, in fact, he begins his letter begging forgiveness of his mentors for a portfolio long on "diversity work" and shorter (than he would like) on anthropological research.

Lanehart's letter presents a real-life scenario about the arbitrary nature of the tenure and promotion process. She describes a situation where those on a P&T committee were *literally* racially and spatially divided, and where she felt she had to advocate for fair treatment for a nonwhite colleague. Her letter is to "African Americans in the Ivory Tower." She says she wants them "to recognize that we have to make a space for our visibility to be in the rooms of power and influence, even at academic institutions that should have faculty and administrators who have been educated out of ignorance, racism, sexism, classism, and all the other -isms that mark small minds."

Our final letter in this section is from an anonymous contributor who tells the tale of being denied promotion and tenure, despite having a twelve-year teaching record at a university. A bitter pill to swallow, to be sure, but in this case, this scholar tells a tale of overcoming the disappointment, embarrassment, and anger to craft a more salubrious and agentic path after this traumatic event.

The section ends with an encouraging and humorous mentor letter from Juan Battle who advises that the "two most important tools to successfully acquiring tenure are the following: (1) get yourself some help, and (2) keep your eyes on the prize." Battle uses personal anecdotes to both illustrate the distractions and challenges faculty can face in the academy, but also how we must, if we are to survive, take practical steps to "do" the work that must be done. It is a hopeful letter—full of practical dos and don'ts—and it reminds us that despite the challenges, faculty of color can and do survive the academy.

REFERENCES

Cole, S. and Barber, E. 2003. *Increasing Faculty Diversity*. Cambridge, MA: Harvard University Press.

Gardner, S. K. 2013. "Women Faculty Departures from a Striving Institution: Between a Rock and a Hard Place." *The Review of Higher Education* 36(3): 349–70.

Harley, D.; Krzys Acord, S.; Earl-Novell, S.; Lawrence, S.; and Judson King. C. 2010. *Assessing the Future Landscape of Scholarly Communication: An Exploration of Faculty Values and Needs in Seven Disciplines*. Berkeley: University of California Press, Center for Studies in Higher Education (CSHE), January. http://escholarship.org/uc/cshe_fsc.

Jones, K.; Beddoes, K.; Banerjee, D.; and Pawley, A. L. 2014. "Examining the Flexibility Bind in American Tenure and Promotion Processes: An Institutional Ethnographic Approach." *Ethnography and Education* 9(3): 328–42.

Joseph, T. and Hirshfield, L. 2010. "'Why Don't You Get Somebody New to Do It?' Race and Cultural Taxation in the Academy." *Ethnic and Racial Studies* 34(1): 121–41.

Misra, J.; Lundquist, J. H.; Holmes, E.; and Agiomavritis, S. 2011. "The Ivory Ceiling of Service Work." *Academe* 97(1): 22–26.

Stanley, C. 2006. "Coloring the Academic Landscape: Faculty of Color Breaking the Silence in Predominantly White Colleges and Universities." *American Educational Research Journal* 43(4): 701–36.

Umbach, P. 2006. "The Contribution of Faculty of Color to Undergraduate Education." *Research in Higher Education* 47(3): 317–45.

Urrieta Jr., L.; Mendez, L.; and Rodriguez, E. 2015. "'A Moving Target': A Critical Race Analysis of Latina/o Faculty Experiences, Perspectives, and Reflections on the Tenure and Promotion Process." *International Journal of Qualitative Studies in Education* 28(10): 1149–68.

Chapter Eight

Letters

LETTER 11

Dear Faculty Members Who Mentor Doctoral Students of Color, (or, Love and Labor in Academia)

I often wonder what it would take for me—a young woman of color—to feel "successful" in academia. On the one hand, the very fact that I have broken through barriers to be a faculty member (that, too, at an Ivy League university) is cause for celebration; on the other hand, I am a member of the contingent and not tenured faculty, and this makes me less successful in the eyes of some.

We academics put a lot of pressure on doctoral students and push them toward tenure-track jobs—that is the prize, and although it is a little different in some fields, the pinnacle of success remains the tenure track. But perhaps we need to redefine what it means to be successful; because not only are the number of available tenure-track positions shrinking year by year, there is also an overproduction of Ph.D.s and Ed.D.s. Concurrently, the contingent faculty workforce is growing by leaps and bounds.

According to the American Association of University Professors (n.d.), more than 50 percent of faculty are contingent faculty, which includes both part- and full-time non-tenure-track faculty, and most of these roles are filled by women (people of color remain a minority both among contingent faculty and tenured faculty). Moreover, more than 75 percent of new instructional staff appointments are now non-tenure track. The pay scale, benefits, and job security can vary from decent to none at all.

For those that do make it to the prized tenure track, the cost is incredibly high, especially for women, and it is compounded further for women of color. Women are more likely than men to make sacrifices related to family life and the pressure that comes with the "publish or perish" mantra does good for no one. In a December 2013 *Guardian* interview, Peter Higgs—the physicist and Nobel prize winner who partly gave his name to the Higgs-Boson particle so important to modern physics—said that no university would hire him today because he would not be considered productive enough (Aitkenhead, 2013). The *quality* of the hyper-production is what really needs to be examined. Too often, the quality of what we publish is signified by the journals we publish in, not by the ideas themselves. Rather than "publish or perish," why do we not attempt to "publish and flourish"?

In addition to this pressure to produce, there is, for many, a growing pressure to accumulate grants. With all of that pressure, we seem to be giving up on the greatest part of what it means to be an academic—at least that is the reason why I always wanted to be an academic—to be a thinker, to contribute new ideas, to push the boundaries of our field, but also to apply our knowledge and add value to the world.

I want to be part of an academia where collaborations and thinking together are celebrated, and where the prize is not the next journal article, but the next big idea. The two are not necessarily synonymous. I do not want to be part of an enterprise where one's identity is so intimately connected to work output (and here, "work output" is defined as the number of scholarly publications and the amount of money that you generate). The root of why and how we've allowed this to happen is in the nature of the path toward a doctoral degree.

Getting your doctorate comes at a great cost—if not always financially, then certainly in the amount of time one must dedicate to its pursuit. And because of this commitment, academics are made to feel that we cannot walk away from it, because how do you walk away from something that inspires so much passion and love? But loving what you do leads you down a slippery slope of what Miya Tokumitsu (2014) calls the "Do What You Love" or DWYL work mantra: "Nothing makes exploitation go down easier than convincing workers that they are doing what they love" (para. 26).

Indeed, my work is emotionally satisfying: it feeds my soul; it makes me incredibly happy. But it is still *work*. I work incredibly hard and I simply cannot forget to acknowledge that and to fight for myself, especially since—as a contingent faculty member of color—the glass ceiling for me is pretty low. In critiquing academia, Sarah Brouillette (2013) argues that "our faith that our work offers nonmaterial rewards, and is more integral to our identity that a 'regular' job would be, makes us ideal employees when the goal of management is to extract our labor's maximum value at minimum cost" (para. 6). As Tokumitsu summarizes, *"We work for social currency rather than real wages"* (para. 28, my emphasis).

All of us young scholars—tenure-track or otherwise, and especially young scholars of color—have been convinced that this is just the way things are and that our research and publications are hard evidence of our love and commitment to our work. The expectations of what an individual is to produce to get tenure today is mind-boggling especially when you compare it to what people just a generation ago needed to be able to get tenure. Scholars of color are expected to prove themselves even more. And the result of this is a very unhealthy way of life.

In 2012, the University and College Union in the United Kingdom released a study that, drawing on a sample of 14,000 university employees, revealed growing stress levels among academics prompted by heavy workloads, a culture that values working long hours, and conflicting management demands. In fact, UCU academics experience higher stress that those in the wider population. In the updated 2014 survey (with a sample of more than 6,000) there was a reported increase in stress levels by a percentage point since 2012.

While there is no similar study in the United States, there have been numerous articles suggesting that this is certainly a worrisome trend here, as well. Moreover, this stress is experienced differently by different subgroup in the academy—those on the tenure track feel it in terms of the "publish or perish" mantra; those who are contingent faculty experience it by the lack of job security and often low pay; and even among these groups, there are differences in how women and people of color experience stress.

Unfortunately, contingent faculty—despite their growing numbers—do not have many allies. We often hear of colleagues on the tenure track who argue that you need to "play by the rules of the game before you can shake up the board." But by the time these supposed allies are in positions of power, they are so often exhausted and sometimes broken by the system that there is little energy left to fight. Tokumitsu (2014) is even less charitable than my summary suggests, and argues that the intense identification between identity and output is why "so many proud left-leaning faculty remain oddly silent about the working conditions of their peers" (para. 21).

Tokumitsu argues that by keeping us focused on ourselves and our individual happiness, the DWYL mantra "distracts us from the working conditions of others while validating our own choices and relieving us from obligations, to all who labor whether or not they love it" (para. 4). Because of our ingrained and gendered belief that we're not doing this for the money, women in particular are victims of this system that extracts female labor for little compensation, but for the greater good—and that is priceless. And again, the burden is even greater for women of color. Nowhere is this labor exploitation seen more than in service work.

In their 2011 article, Earle Reybold and Kirstan Corda talk about the significant service burden that faculty of color bear, resulting in "cultural taxation," characterized by Padilla (1994) as "the obligation to show good citizenship toward the institution by serving its needs for ethnic representation on committees or to demonstrate knowledge and commitment to a cultural group" (p. 26). In this way, scholars of color are often seen as representative of an entire group while whites are typically seen as individuals. In other words, people of color bear the burden of representation in a way that white people never have to, and since the academy remains majority white, this perspective continues to thrive.

As Reybold and Corda (2011) argue, the institution is rewarded for its attention to diversity while the faculty members performing the services are not, especially since most service work continues to be seen as outside the realm of the "real work" that scholars do. While service work is a burden of sorts for all academics, it is without question a burden borne more by women and other minority faculty who are made to feel that they have to prove something extra to legitimize their being there.

Because issues of diversity, and particularly racial diversity, are so central to a university's prestige and "mission" these days, just like students of color, so too are faculty of color a tangible display of a school's diversity and at times, even the institutions' commitment to social justice. Minority status then becomes the lens through which scholars of color are viewed. Every action and nonaction taken by a faculty of color is scrutinized in a way that white faculty members almost never experience—especially white, straight male faculty.

As Ella Shohat (1995) explains, when you're in the majority, there are lots of different representations and so any negative behavior or image is just seen as an individual act and part of the natural diversity. Therefore, members of the dominant group need not preoccupy themselves too much with being adequately represented.

For example, if a white faculty member does not do as much service work or slacks a little, the individual is criticized. But if a faculty of color indulges in the same kind of behavior, the criticism extends beyond the individual to the group. Shohat (1995) states, "Representation of an underrepresented group is necessarily within the hermeneutics of domination, overcharged with allegorical significance" (170). In other words, since representations of the marginalized are few, the few available are thought to be representative of all marginalized people. This is the academic status quo that penalizes both women and people of color. Our success not only depends on *what* we "produce" but also *how* we participate in service work.

If that is what academia is to remain, then it may not be the place for me in the long run. My letter here, then, is a plea for us to reimagine what we want academia to look like and to redefine what it means to be a "successful" academic. Not only the quality of our work, but also our own health depends on it.

I want to end with Tokumitsu (2014) again, because she makes such a powerful plea: "If we acknowledge all of our work as work, we could set appropriate limits for it, demanding fair compensation and humane schedules that allow for family and leisure time. And if we did that, more of us could get around to doing what it is we really love" (para. 32).

With regards,
Ameena Ghaffar-Kucher

REFERENCES

Aitkenhead, Decca. (2013). "Peter Higgs: I Wouldn't Be Productive Enough for Today's Academic System." *The Guardian*, December 6. http://www.theguardian.com/science/2013/dec/06/peter-higgs-boson-academic-system. Accessed September 30, 2015.

American Association of University Professors. (n.d.). "Background Facts on Contingent Faculty." http://www.aaup.org/issues/contingency/background-facts. Accessed September 30, 2015.

Brouillette, S. 2013. "Academic Labor, the Aesthetics of Management, and the Promise of Autonomous Work." http://nonsite.org/article/academic-labor-the-aesthetics-of-management-and-the-promise-of-autonomous-work. Accessed October 30, 2015.

Reybold, E. and Corda, K. 2011. "Faculty Identity and the 'Lesser Role': Service to the Academy." *Journal of the Professoriate* 5(1): 121–48.

Shohat, Ella. 1995. "The Struggle over Representation: Casting, Coalitions, and the Politics of Identification." In Roman de la Campa, E.; Ann Kaplan; and Michael Sprinkler (eds.), *Late Imperial Culture*. New York: Verso.

Tokumitsu, Miya. 2014. "In the Name of Love." *Jacobin*, Issue 13. https://www.jacobinmag.com/2014/01/in-the-name-of-love/. Accessed September 30, 2015.

University and College Union. 2012. "2012 UCU Stress Survey." http://www.ucu.org.uk/stresssurvey12. Accessed September 30, 2015.

University and College Union. 2014. "USC Survey of Work-Related Stress 2014." http://www.ucu.org.uk/media/pdf/t/e/ucu_festressreport14.pdf. Accessed September 30, 2015.

LETTER 12

Dear Friends and Colleagues,

This is an apology to all those professors and mentors who believed in me, who encouraged me, and who told me I had the makings of a good anthropologist. Sorry I stopped exploring that potential. Sorry I got distracted. Sorry you haven't seen my name in print lately.

I had a dream: I'd commit to anthropology, fieldwork, writing, and making a useful contribution to knowledge. I studied gender and fundamentalist religion. These two things, when mixed, can squash a lot of people's dreams—mostly women's. I dreamed that I would study that quandary, help solve it, and leave the world a little better than I found it.

Except I haven't made any progress toward my dream since I became a professor. I've been busy with "diversity" work.

I'm among a few fortunate professors who have managed to turn a one-year appointment into a tenure-track position. I should be, and largely am, quite happy to be employed. State universities like mine have had budgets gutted, employees' salaries frozen, and are ordered to produce more, without raising students' tuition. That's higher education in the 21st century: certainly an oppressive system.

So I walked into this oppressive system, dream in my back pocket, looking to make a difference. That's the equivalent of having an iron chain knotted around your neck while offering the loose end to any passersby willing to snatch it. At least, it seems to be, if you look like me.

Minnesota State Colleges and Universities (MNSCU) are not renowned for having a diverse faculty. Bringing in the brown son of Central American immigrants counts as a rare win for them. Within weeks of my arrival, many folks showed up at my door, willing to snatch at the chain around my neck, leading me from event to event, initiative to initiative, acronym to acronym (every diversity group seems to require a brand new acronym) in an attempt to . . . what? Make me visible? Get me "involved"? Help me feel welcome?

I'm not sure of the intent, or where they set out to lead me. I do know where I ended up: back at my desk, with a giant stack of paperwork that had nothing to do with anthropology, my classes, or adding to a body of knowledge. I sat, often licking wounds from a nasty "diversity confrontation," anxiously drafting invites so more than five people showed up to a diversity event, or hurriedly writing out the food order for it. I became a beast-of-burden for any campus effort involving race, gender, religion . . . and so on. I wanted to make a difference.

In short, my university has a serious "diversity problem," and I was conveniently available to do something about it. The school itself can (as of 2015) boast that it has 38 percent students of color. (Take that, universities boasting that their 10 percent means they are diverse.) However, it has those numbers because it's the cheapest, most flexible game in town, with plenty of night classes for the working adult.

The school did not recruit students of color, of diverse religions, of non-conforming gender, nor did it prepare an infrastructure that meets their needs. They end up here in droves because it lay within their reach. Schools scramble in situations like that, appointing inexperienced guys like me to diversity organizations without a clear purpose or budget to execute plans.

There were already plenty of initiatives on campus that were also unfunded and disorganized, and absolutely convinced that their methods work. They've been trying for fifteen years, but still haven't achieved instituting a program of mandatory diversity training for all incoming faculty and staff, a program for training for tutors working with English language learners, a working Diversity Plan, orientation programs preparing students for diverse classrooms, programs preparing nontraditional students for traditional professors, or systems tracking statistical outcomes for our most vulnerable students, staff, and faculty.

Pointing these issues out, however, leads to further tightening of the iron noose around one's neck. My anthropological analysis, informed by feminism and cultural relativism, was not welcome. "Ethnocentrism," unfortunately, applies to too many things schools are used to doing. I was resented.

Just because the students reflect various colors and creeds doesn't mean professors, staff, or administrators know how to deal with them. I don't just mean your stereotypical "over-educated, white privilege–having, elitist, racist bigot," though they certainly exist. I also mean zealous antiracist allies who alienate others with their anger, well-intended administrators who attended a white privilege conference once and seek to alleviate guilt, and staff who have twenty years' experience and "welcomed" the diversity when it "happened." No one likes hearing what they're doing isn't enough, or that what they've done hasn't worked, or that they still don't "get it."

"Diversity" involves a lot of people refusing to believe their ideas and approaches are part of the problem, not the solution. A professor avowing that black immigrant students dislike her because they "have a problem with strong women" only sounds like feminism if you're selling discount feminism. Departmental insistence that says letting a student of color graduate serves the cause of racial justice, despite the student's inability to write in complete sentences, pass exams, or meet requirements, ignores the fact that you just sent a vulnerable graduate into an unforgiving racist society. Yet for me to challenge a professor speaking as a feminist, or a department's commitment to racial justice, welcomes a violent response.

The worst attacks I've suffered have come from other people of color. Like me, they probably got thrown into this lion's den years ago, and kept rabidly biting at everyone around them, trying to make a difference. Now, they'll bite at anything just to feel the reassuring strength of their own jaws. Once, a faculty leader privately visited to discuss official charges being filed against me (an immigrant and person of color) by an influential and allegedly antiracist department chair and full professor. I had contradicted this person in a meeting by suggesting that focusing solely on race in university matters ignores other forms of oppression. The faculty leader told me not to worry, as this particular professor "does this all the time."

It's a trauma response. Many white antiracists and people of color have experienced discrimination so often that they throw frequent fits. Since racism exists everywhere, there is always something to attack. They "challenge" anything or anyone they can, then justify it as a solemn duty. One result: the words "diversity" and "antiracism" receive a collective groan as many of our employees and students equate them with the barks and howls of rabid dogs. No one really wants to cooperate with the "diversity guy" if they've come to believe he's of an ilk likely to bite them—or bring them up on charges for disagreeing with him. My predecessors' trauma stacked the cards against me before I got here.

So here's a short list of things that have wasted my time and distracted me from my dream in the last five years:

- Early on, two white faculty approached me separately to inform me where the best burritos in town are.
- Two older Latinos brought me to the Latino Caucus, then excluded me when they discovered I am of Guatemalan and Honduran descent, not Mexican American.
- A native-born member of the Latino Caucus snidely remarked, "Oh god, the immigrants are here to save us," when I suggested marketing more toward immigrants.
- A white colleague sent me a job posting at another university, with the message, "I think this place is more like what you're looking for" when I'd suggested organizing an event on conflict between groups in the workplace.
- "Great performance! Just what we needed," said a dean after I challenged a student's public slur that my colleague "did not count" as Native American, since she (though of native parentage) was not registered with a tribe. This same dean had also been present, but said nothing.
- Interviewing another potential anthropology hire, a senior member of my department remarked as I left early, "He's a Latino lover. He's probably off to another date."
- Our support staff, after I jimmied open her drawer lock with a pocket knife, said, "Glad we've got a Puerto Rican with a switchblade ready!"
- The faculty president explained to me that he understood all my difficulties, since he has a German heritage.

And so on. I've got an itchy feeling these things wouldn't have occurred if I were white. I don't really have time to explore the idea, since I have to prepare for a workshop on social inclusion to be held this Friday.

Many might argue that I've achieved my dream. Someone in those ill-attended workshops and events may have felt empowered. I get e-mails and tearful visits from grateful students and employees. Perhaps I'm just disappointed the file I have marked "Scholarly Work" is so thin. I could've done more research, written more. I sacrificed that time and effort to the Diversity Gods of Minnesota State. I thought I could make a difference. I don't know if I really have.

I'm a tenured professor now. Turns out a file folder marked "Service to the University" lent some bulk to my tenure dossier. That means I got a raise and I can ignore people when they threaten to get me fired. Maybe that's the silver lining in all this: job security. So, sorry I haven't produced much anthropology lately. I was busy buying the freedom to do it at my own pace.

Sincerely,
Jose

LETTER 13

Dear Colleagues, (or, Being in the Room)

As a Full Professor and Endowed Chair, one might think I have proven my credentials and that my scholarship is beyond reproach. However, I am an African American woman and we are never beyond reproach. (I learned that even applies to Toni Morrison, one of the most brilliant writers to have ever written. More on that later.) I have learned that lesson over and over, hoping for something different; however, I am told that is the definition of insanity.

I lost faith in the power of higher education and intellectualism long ago. When I was much younger, I believed that education was the answer to many societal ills. Unemployed or underemployed? Education. Racism and all the other -isms? Education. Injustice and inequity? Education.

Unfortunately, education is not the answer. Higher education is a reflection of society, not an ivory tower removed from it. If there is bigotry in society, there is bigotry in higher education. If there is racism in society, there is racism in higher education. If there is anti-intellectualism in society, there is anti-intellectualism in higher education. Education does not allow one to escape or rise above the everyday.

Being African American trumps benefit-of-the-doubt expectations. We need only look at the actions against President Barack Obama: birthers, scores of votes to repeal the Affordable Care Act, a congressman yelling "you lie" at the State of the Union address, being told he is articulate as if it is a surprise, dismissing or attacking his Ivy League education, and questioning his right to belong in the office. Like President Obama, at every step, my intellect, ability, and leadership have been scrutinized.

Despite my position and credentials, faculty in my department have been allowed to interrogate my credentials and evaluate my work on multiple occasions as if I were going through the tenure and promotion process (with the exception of gathering external letters of support). Including one post-tenure review, I have been reviewed by my department faculty four times in less than nine years. After the second review, I found solace and direction in Lucille Clifton's 1983 poem "Won't You Celebrate with Me" and made it my e-mail signature. Most poignant are the last four few lines.

In spite of it all, I am a vocal advocate for social justice and equity because I do not believe there is a "right time" to work toward our needs. "Waiting until _____ (Ph.D. in hand, tenure-track job, tenure and promotion to associate professor, another book, another grant, promotion to full professor, etc.)" is not the answer because there is always something more that can be done or achieved to make you feel as though you have proven yourself, that you have arrived, that you are not an impostor. As an African American woman, that script is played every day: "When will I arrive at the point when my work, my intellect, my leadership, and my accomplishments are worthy and are enough? When do I get to finally arrive? When do I get to be free and black every day?"

The most recent event that brings me to writing this letter involves an important institutional activity gone wrong: the tenure and promotion process. We all knew there would be contention involved, but I did not expect the level of unprofessional, disrespectful, and unmitigated gall that showed itself.

In the room itself, faculty of color and their allies sat together on one side of the table and white faculty sat together on the other side of the table. On several occasions, I had to raise my voice to say, "This is not in the files. This is not procedure. This is not ethical. This is not legal. This is despicable." The microaggressions and racism were palpable and intolerable. It was as if I was floating above the room watching an unspeakable event since it could not be possible that such highly educated people could speak and think in such ignorant, problematic, and unprofessional ways.

At one point, one of the senior, white, male faculty read from a manuscript in progress by the candidate and noted a subject-verb agreement error. He would have gone on had he not been stopped. Who does something like that in an institutional evaluative setting? When one of the senior, white, female faculty, under her breath, suggested that Toni Morrison was not the acclaimed writer people make her out to be, I knew I was done because, if Toni Morrison has not "made it," the rest of us don't stand a chance.

During another point, an unremarkable and underachieving tenured faculty member who has not even met the minimum credentials for tenure being espoused was the most vocal. Though she herself does not have the requisite solo-authored book on her CV, she was counting pages of the accepted book manuscript by a top publisher in the field. She questioned the competence of the candidate to revise according to the publisher feedback. She and her allies were actually trying to calculate the percentage of pages that would need to be revised.

At another point, I felt as though we were back at President Bill Clinton's impeachment hearing where he questioned what "is" is. There were faculty debating if the submitted and accepted manuscript was actually a book even though the publisher and their reviewers as well as the external reviewers believed it was. Where was all this scrutiny when the unremarkable faculty member went through the process?

After leaving that meeting and being physically ill for two days (I still feel mentally wounded), I was able to gain clarity after talking to my mother (as usual). In retelling the incident, I noticed she was having difficulty grasping what I was articulating. As I have conveyed myriad incidents to my mom about academia, she finally stated in this case that she struggled with the situation because in her day, African Americans were not allowed to be in the room for the types of situations I have described to her (e.g., tenure and promotion cases, leadership, etc.). African Americans were simply told the results and what to do as they were being taken care of by "the white folk." Now I understood: we are invisible even when we make it to the room because we were never expected to be in the room, much less in the front.

I write this letter to African Americans in the ivory tower to recognize that we have to make a space for our visibility to be in the rooms of power and influence even at academic institutions that should have faculty and administrators who have been educated out of ignorance, racism, sexism, classism, and all the other -isms that mark small minds. We have been told that things will get better soon as the old guard dies out. However, I have learned that they exemplify one of the catchphrases from the 1992 film *Bébé's Kids*: they don't die, they multiply.

Finally, I want to remind you that, though it may sound cliché, it's not you, it's them. African Americans in the ivory tower are not the problem. The final tenure and promotion activity that clarified this fact for me was in cochairing the college-level committee and hearing one of the senior faculty say, "It doesn't matter what we do. The fix is in." We knew in that space that it was not about merit, accolades, and survival of the fittest.

Just think of the Abigail Fisher affirmative action case. It is okay to be white and mediocre, but it is not okay to be African American and mediocre. So, know that just by being in the room, you are already better. By being in the room, the presence of your light reveals the darkness of racism and we all know that light makes the dark scatter.

Sincerely,
Sonja Lanehart

REFERENCES

Clifton, L. 1983. "Won't You Celebrate with Me?" http://www.dailymotion.com/video/xgkhun_lucille-clifton-won-t-you-celebrate-with-me_creation. Accessed July 28, 2015.
"President Bill Clinton's Impeachment Hearing." https://www.youtube.com/watch?v=j4XT-l-_3y0. Accessed December 22, 2007.

LETTER 14

Dear Colleagues, (or, Liberation and the Denial of an Academic Career)

I was attending a homecoming football game on the campus of a well-respected New England university where my eldest child attended college when my cell phone rang. On the other end of the receiver was the dean for the sciences and arts division at the university where I taught. I knew his call had to do with my bid for tenure, so I stepped away from the group and readied myself for the decision when I heard him apologize before delivering the news. I learned that after successfully negotiating all the previous departmental and college hurdles, I had been denied tenure by the provost of the university. All I could do was give him a chipper "thank you for the call," and hang up. What was supposed to be a celebratory fall weekend instead marked the unceremonious end of my academic career as an African American woman in cultural anthropology.

I had spent a total of twelve years at this university—five as a full time, temporary instructor, and then as a tenure-eligible assistant professor after my first book was published. During the six-year period leading to the submission of my tenure file, I published peer-reviewed journal articles, collaborated on community-based research projects, worked with grassroots organizations whose foci paralleled my research concerns, and helped establish ties between the university and the local community.

By all accounts, based on the assessments of peers and students, not only was I making key contributions to the social sciences with my focus on the dynamic, layered, and, sometimes, contradictory ways race and class shaped the experiences of African American people living in cities, I was also an effective teacher and I enhanced the reputation of the department nationwide as the result of my media appearances. Potential students paid attention to these appearances and, once they got to campus, I regularly made myself available to advise students. Finally, even as the president of the university was rejecting my appeal of his provost's decision, I had received and signed a contract to have my second book published, and this was a fact my department head was sure to make known to the upper administration.

In the end, neither my teaching, research, or service record described above, nor the evaluations of the tenure committee (an impartial group of scholars who deemed my body of work groundbreaking and important to urban anthropology) were enough to sway the two powerful actors in whose hands the final decision rested. The conclusions documented by those who supported my tenure bid were completely disregarded by two white men who knew the least about the content and import of my research, teaching, and service to my department and the larger university.

The university president went on record with the conclusion that my scholarly efforts did not meet the standards of his institution. I was defeated, and rather than return for the final semester of my contract, I submitted my letter of resignation and declined to attend any of the "goodbye" parties my former colleagues attempted to throw together.

Being denied tenure after more than a decade at this institution left me numb. Many people were taken aback by the decision and, in the wake of this verdict, students began organizing in protest. One undergraduate student wrote an article in the student paper that included a gigantic photograph of my face on the cover. Graduate students put a Facebook page together, and as the process progressed, a small group went to talk to the university president to advocate for the provost's decision to be reversed.

In the meantime I consulted a lawyer and, because the absence of a second book was the only stated reason why I was not granted tenure and I had a publisher's contract in hand, this attorney felt we had a pretty good case against the school. The lawyer further indicated that the costs to retain his services were steep; additional fees would accumulate over time and he would not be able to take my case on contingency. After considering my options, I chose not to pursue a lawsuit against the university and became unemployed at the end of the spring semester in 2011.

Losing my job gave me a sense of both panic and relief. My identity was closely intertwined with my work as a college professor. I took on contracting work and was hired as an adjunct professor at a nearby university. I also continued to consult on community-based research projects and began constructing and seeking funding for projects of my own. I also had more time to promote my second book.

Of course, the inevitable occurred. People asked, "What do you do?" When I was socializing with academics, they wanted to know "Where do you teach?" My patented response became, "I am an independent scholar." In my mind, "independent scholar" was a polite euphemism for saying I was jobless. However, something profound happened when I was asked where I taught after making the acquaintance of some anthropologists who were visiting D.C. to attend the annual professional meetings of 2014. I felt good—even powerful in responding, "I am an independent scholar" and my confidence must have been contagious because the person asking the question smiled and nodded as if she always knew what I was just beginning to realize. I was not without power.

To be clear, being fired from your job is not an event to shrug off or take lightly in any way. Unemployment, whether anticipated or sudden, can result in economic disaster. My situation, however was exceptional and fortunate. My spouse was able to pick up the economic slack and compensate for the loss of my approximately $79,000 annual salary as well as the health and other benefits I had earned as an assistant professor. The rejection I received was disheartening, but in time I began to imagine the emancipatory aspects of what otherwise was a huge barrier in the progression of my professional development.

Needless to say, when the fall 2012 semester began and I didn't have to teach, my schedule opened up significantly. Now, I had the time to take on my own projects—a shift that allowed me to explore untapped aspects of my earlier work, skills, and interests. Oddly enough, this experience presented me with an opportunity for growth and as a middle-aged educator/scholar, I began to ponder the meaning of these personal shifts. I had to face and deliberate over what I sincerely wanted at this juncture in my life cycle. I also had the time to search for a job that had meaning for me and that resonated with the professional lessons I had learned up to that point.

In addition to these philosophical concerns, I was also liberated from the parade of microaggressions I had endured for years teaching courses on racism and African American culture. While I had experienced profoundly rewarding encounters in the classroom, I also contended with hostility, privilege, and resentment as represented by the bevy of offensive, in-class remarks that I had to either dispassionately respond to or magically transform into "teachable moments."

Included among these were such comments suggesting that black women are lazy and that is why there are such high rates of obesity; that affirmative action is a form of racism; that black women have ugly big butts; that it is unfair that only African Americans can call other African Americans "nigger"; that black people make everything about race. Once I was even told that I was racist because I told a black student that she had made a good comment but I didn't say the same to a particular white student that same day.

I often faced a cavalcade of distrust, discomfort, and anger that would bubble up at the most surprising moments. One semester, my window was shattered after I confronted students who my teaching assistants informed me had cheated on an introductory cultural anthropology course by using those personal information devices that preceded the invention of the smartphone.

In hindsight, teaching the types of courses I was assigned to a largely white, middle-class student body was a terribly stressful experience. The disappointments of being denied tenure notwithstanding, three years later I have come to understand that confronting the weekly expressions of entitlement and bigotry was damaging to my psyche and intellectual development. Today, I am basking in the belief that 2016 is going to lead me to a second and very satisfying career. I have taken what the academy had to teach me and have given much in return. Losing my job as a college professor has presented me with a future that I am certain will deliver great dividends in the coming years.

Moving forward,
Anonymous

Chapter Nine

Mentor Essay

Tenure

Juan Battle, City University of New York (CUNY)

It has been said that audiences are most likely to remember the first and last thing you tell them. Therefore, I want to make sure not to bury my lede. In my opinion, the two most important tools to successfully acquiring tenure are the following: (1) get yourself some help, and (2) keep your eyes on the prize.

I received my Ph.D. and started my first tenure-track job in 1994. Like most senior faculty, I have written more tenure letters of recommendation than I care to remember: so many letters, that it has become easier and easier to see who received (or at least heeded) good mentoring and who did not.

A dear friend and junior colleague likes to recount a brief, yet poignant, interaction he and I had some years ago, when he was an assistant professor. He called me while I was rushing to an important meeting. I hastily took his call. I answered the phone in my rush and impatience, yet I still wanted to be helpful. The conversation went like this:

Juan: Hey Joe, I'm kinda busy. What's up?

Joe: Juan, I have a situation I need you to help me think through.

Juan: Is it personal or professional?

Joe: Professional.

Juan: The answer is tenure. BYE!

And then I quickly hung up the phone.

89

I knew that my response would not land as harshly for him as it might for others. I knew this because over many years, he and I had had numerous conversations about tenure, the tenure process, and short-term versus long-term goals, as well as the business versus the B.S. (and I don't mean bachelor of science) of higher education.

Through conversations over the phone as well as at hotel bars during conferences, we had already discussed the relative importance of research, teaching, and service in the enterprise of tenure acquisition.

So in these remarks, I thought I'd share the highlights of some of those conversations.

RESEARCH

During my tenure as a professor, I've worked on projects and grants as small as a few thousand dollars and as large as a few million; and many publications as well.

Like most doctoral candidates, I came out of graduate school not knowing how to publish articles or write grants. However, I identified senior colleagues who were kind and patient enough to sit with me as I learned from them.

Concerning getting help, it's as I tell my graduate students: "When it comes to your research, it's a dissertation and not masturbation . . . don't do it by yourself. Get yourself some help." As a junior faculty member, develop a community of people—both inside and outside of your institution—who are invested in your success.

"Publish or perish" is so ubiquitous a mandate that it borders on cliché. However, far too many junior faculty don't start thinking strategically about what it means until after their third-year review—at which point, let's face it, they're already behind.

Also, and let me be clear here, the phrase is "*publish* or perish"; it is not "do research or be removed."

When you go up for tenure, the distinction between those phrases is not semantic, it's seismic. Assistant professors who spend their time (only) going to conferences, (only) workshopping their articles and chapters, (only) participating in writing groups, (only) thinking deeply about their work . . . will NOT get tenure. Yes, all of those steps are important—and yes, I have at times undertaken all of those steps. But at some point, that work has to be sent out for blind peer review. You have to read and incorporate comments from people who don't know (and often don't care) about you; your course load; your gender, race, or sexual orientation. They are critically commenting on your work.

Therefore, long before that powerful phone call with Joe, he and I had already discussed that publications and grants are the currency that purchase you favor in the academy. He knew that the majority of faculty negotiate with their dean about receiving more money for travel, or course releases; while a precious few of us are able to discuss percentage returns on overhead, indirect costs, and/or institutional matching. I had already told Joe that although the second set of conversations might (at times) be more contentious, it is those conversations and the necessity for them that will put a candidate in a strengthened position for tenure.

It is easy to push research—which to me includes both publications *and* grantsmanship—off. Teaching happens twice a week (if you're lucky). There's a room full of people waiting for you; thus you have to prepare for them. But when it comes to publications, you can keep telling yourself that you'll work on them "over the break." When I was a junior faculty member, I "did" my teaching during the semester and "worked" on my teaching during the semester breaks; conversely, writing and running grants happened year-round.

TEACHING

Over my career, I have taught more undergraduate and graduate courses than I can name. Suffice it to say that my classes have been as small as eight and as large as 300. I've taught everything from Introduction to Sociology to advanced methods and statistics courses at the Ph.D. level. I've had teaching assistants, and I've had to go it alone. I've had some incredibly bright students and I've had some (umm) who (umm) were not. My point? I bring a wide range of experience to the topic of teaching.

As a junior faculty member, you don't have to be stellar. You just make sure you don't suck. Budget your time accordingly. Based on our conversations, Joe knew this meant that you only have to grade what you assign. Joe also knew that teaching evaluations in the top 90th percentile will get you praise, but won't—in and of themselves—get you promoted.

Earlier, I said that I "did" my teaching during the semester and "worked" on my teaching during the semester breaks. Let me take a minute and unpack that. As much as was humanly possible, teaching was reduced to meeting with students during the actual semester. The time and mental energy I put into teaching was minimal because everything was already developed and locked into place during the breaks.

By "worked" on teaching, I mean reading and deciding how to incorporate new material, preparing syllabi, making copies, finding out when grants were due (and thus I knew there were certain periods when I'd need more time to write; that's when I'd show films and line up guest speakers). Once the semester started, nothing changed on the syllabus, enough copies (including of the midterm and final exams) were already made, guest speakers were already lined up, etcetera. Things were in place so that all I had to do was grab my teaching folder for that class session and everything was in it, ready to go.

I was, and still am, a *huge* fan of student peer review when it comes to grading. Therefore, when I was an assistant professor, for my smaller classes (with 40 or fewer students), students would bring in three copies of drafts of their assignments and, for homework, comment on their colleagues' papers. Those papers would be returned, comments incorporated, and then I would see the final paper. For (many, though not all of) my graduate courses, which tend to have about 20 students, they would have two rounds of peer review . . . all before I saw the final product. Executing this procedure takes preparation and clarity of instruction; however, it makes grading the final product much easier and intellectually digestible.

Also, when it comes to teaching, get your ego out of the way. Let's face it: those students really don't want to come to class three hours a week for fifteen weeks to hear your voice. Just because you may be the most knowledgeable voice in the room (on that subject), does not mean you're the most interesting. I'm a fan of student presentations, in both "content" and "methods" courses.

Finally, don't be afraid to structure your class so that it helps you get your work published. Develop assignments that are somehow linked to your research. For students who want to do independent studies, have them independently help you study your research. In exchange, be open to putting their names on a (conference) paper or something. Just because it's their independent study doesn't mean it can't serve your agenda.

SERVICE

This can easily become a time pit and a distraction. When you are a junior faculty member, faculty, staff, and students will reach out to you for a variety of reasons. Some will come to recruit and incorporate you into their organizations and causes; others, to inspect you; and a few, to exterminate you. Until you get tenure, I would serve on ONE departmental committee and ONE institutional committee each year. For every other committee, while smiling, I would say "Thank you for thinking of me; but I am teaching and working (on an article, book, grant). As much as I'd like to partner with you on that committee, at this stage of my career, I really need to prioritize those other items and tenure."

By the way, avoid serving on hiring committees. They are full of landmines that eat an enormous amount of time and provide no guaranteed return on your investment. I know it feeds the ego to be on a committee that will shape the future of the department. But your not getting tenure will *also* shape the future of the department.

MISCELLANEOUS

Here I want to address three things that I've seen serve as major roadblocks to (racial, gender, and sexual minorities) faculty getting tenure.

1. Conferences

If you go to a conference, don't use it solely as a reason to spend fifteen minutes on a dais presenting your work to ten people. As a junior faculty member, use it as an opportunity to network with senior colleagues and funders. In advance of the conference, schedule at least ten 15 minute one-on-one sessions with people who will help you get to the next level. More often than not, those people are not going to go to your session, so you will have to go theirs. Develop your social capital. Meet one-on-one with potential funders, even if your research is in its nascence. Find out whose work is funded for $500,000 or more and attend their sessions. Trust me, other well-funded scholars will be at that session as well.

2. Microaggressions

Much has been written on this topic. I particularly like the point that no aggression is micro. However, when it comes to getting tenure, don't major in the minor. If a colleague comes into your life or a student comes into your class as a bigot, they'll probably leave that way. If they came in ignorant, you can expose them to information that may (or may not) educate them. Either way, that's not your problem or your job. You're their colleague or professor, not their therapist or life coach.

3. Hostile Work Environments

Here are my top five suggestions for working in a hostile work environment. To be honest, though I claim they're mine, I've "borrowed" and "collapsed" them from many of my mentors over the years.

    a. Don't expect to be appreciated. You took the job to be paid, not appreciated. If you want appreciation, look to your family and friends—not your colleagues.

    b. Don't let your environment get inside of you. A boat and water are fine working together, as long as the boat stays in the water. When the water gets in the boat, then there's trouble. Make sure the water that is supposed to be *around* you does not get *in* you. How do you know if it's in you? If you are angry and/or bitter, then some got in. Bail it out!

c. Where you are does not define where you are going. You might be a junior professor and/or at a school you don't like right now. However, that does not mean you (will) have to stay at that level or place for the rest of your life. Pay your dues, do your job well, keep your eyes on your long-term future and not your short-term situation.

d. Do not pledge allegiance to cliques in your workplace. This one is self-explanatory.

e. Don't forfeit your joy. I have been told time and time again that my laugh is large, loud, and obnoxious. Well, so is *my* joy. Actually, it's not obnoxious to people who affirm and love me—and I don't look for affirmation or love on my job (see letter "a" above).

I've covered quite a bit in this essay. But let me end where I began: (1) get yourself some help, and (2) keep your eyes on the prize. I hope that by your taking the time to read this, I too have made a (small) investment in your success. Make sure we all—you included—get a return!

IV

Administration

Chapter Ten

Literature on Administrative Contexts with Focus on Recruitment and Retention

Though both groups work for institutions of higher learning, faculty and administrators are often put at odds. Perhaps it is because the notion of what it means to work for the greater good of a university is such a broad one: despite this common goal, employees of the same institution may work at cross-purposes. As the letters in this section show, such tensions are often exacerbated for faculty of color. Tensions in three areas—recruitment, retention, and recognition—are addressed in this brief research summary.

Despite decades of diversity efforts, faculty of color are underrepresented in the academy. In 2013 (the most recent year for which data is available), there were 1.5 million faculty (full- and part-time) in degree-granting post-secondary institutions: 51 percent were full-time and 49 percent were part-time. Of all full-time faculty, 79 percent were white (43 percent were white males and 35 percent were white females), 6 percent were black, 5 percent were Hispanic, and 10 percent were Asian/Pacific Islander. American Indian/Alaska Native and individuals claiming two or more races make up the smallest groups; each are less than 1 percent of the U.S. faculty population (U.S. Department of Education, 2015).

As indicated in the figure below, among full-time professors, 84 percent were white (58 percent were white males and 26 percent were white females), 4 percent were black, 3 percent were Hispanic, and 9 percent were Asian/Pacific Islander. Making up less than 1 percent each were professors who were American Indian/Alaska Native and of two or more races.

A lack of campus diversity (student and faculty) can be viewed as a lack of departmental/university/administrative effort to recruit, hire, and retain

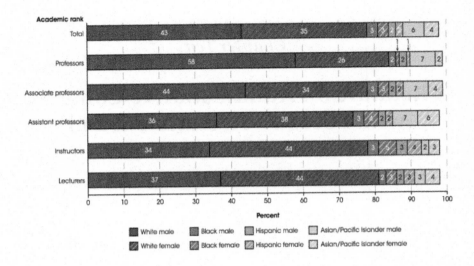

Figure 10.1. Percentage distribution of full-time instructional faculty in degree-granting postsecondary institutions, by academic rank, selected race/ethnicity, and sex: Fall 2013.

NOTE: Degree-granting institutions grant associate's or higher degrees and participate in Title IV federal financial aid programs. Race categories exclude persons of Hispanic ethnicity. Estimates are based on full-time faculty whose race/ethnicity was known. Detail may not sum to 100 percent because data on some racial/ethnic groups are not shown.

faculty of color. Administration is often savvy enough to know that it extracts a special "value-added" benefit from faculty of color on campus. Faculty of color provide countless hours of free advice, often to students who are not formally enrolled in that professor's class. According to recent literature in *The Chronicle of Higher Education* (June 2015), faculty of color are frequently overburdened with responsibilities that are not effectively articulated within existing promotion and tenure matrices that stress the three primary categories of research/writing, teaching, and service.

Administrators are the actors who implement the policies of the university that tax faculty of color. Many university administrations have been effective in designing sleek literature and website pages professing their dedication to diversity. Notwithstanding these public relations efforts that emphasize the intangibles that professors of color add to the campus environment, it is often still a struggle to convince these same administrations to dedicate tangible resources such as grant monies, course releases, teaching assistants, and the like to their professors of color (Ashraf and Shabbir, 2006).

Administrators should be well aware that the advice and inspiration doled out by faculty of color to their diverse student body often play a role in student retention. By failing to acknowledge these social dynamics, many administrators effectively render the faculty of color invisible. The irony is that faculty of color are highly visible as minorities on campus, yet invisible when it comes to access and control over university resources.

More and more, administrators extol the virtues of a more efficient, corporate-run campus (complete with bonus incentives for university presidents) to ensure long-term viability (de Boer, 2015). The corporatization process results from the accumulation of pressures that make funding higher education a more precarious experience. Provided this dynamic continues (and, in light of sweeping, state-level budget cuts negatively impacting public university coffers, it seems as if it will), pressure will only continue to mount for the university to be run efficiently the way any large, sprawling, influential business should be. In times such as these, efforts for more inclusive (more equitable) campuses may be sidelined as too costly.

However, research indicates that faculty of color are shouldering a disproportionate share of the cost for inclusion. Of note, while it is encouraging to see people of color gain access to higher-level administrative positions (e.g., presidents and deans) as well as middle-tier administrative positions (chief diversity officers, center directors) and support staff (department assistants, etc.) who seek to lessen the cultural taxation of faculty of color, researchers posit that many administrators of color likely endure such taxation themselves (Chun and Evans, 2012; Joseph and Hirshfield, 2011).

Research that directly focuses on relationships between administration and faculty of color is surprisingly sparse. Yet, a large body of research addresses topics that require administrative response (Turner, González, and Wood, 2008). These include the need to institutionalize diversity goals (Chesler and Young Jr., 2015; Williams and Wade-Golden, 2007), develop supportive administrative leadership (González, 2007), and create opportunities for mentoring, collegial networks, and collaborative communities (Dixon-Reeves, 2003; Williams, 2007).

The letters in this section reflect the challenges of navigating relations with academic administrations. Ani's letter reminds us of the power of the word "dignity," and the difficulty involved in remaining true to oneself. Her account suggests that many nonwhite academics endure a painful process of self-mutilation, being asked to be complicit in the public denial of their true identities just in order to "go along to get along" within the existing power structure.

Duhaney's letter then challenges us to reconsider the merits of contorting and muting one's racial identity to better fit in. In this case, Duhaney examines an instance when student evaluations only serve to mutilate professional dignity, as these pieces of feedback are one mechanism whereby an individual without an undergraduate degree can trump one with a Ph.D. For better or for worse, administration takes the concerns of frustrated students very seriously—even those concerns based upon race and not based within reality.

Gilliams then details a harrowing account of attempting to be an effective advocate for students of color on campus, only to be condescendingly instructed to "temper your rhetoric." Gilliams's letter raises the question of when it is permitted to raise one's voice in defense of the defenseless. What does one do when reprimanded on the job for doing one's job? Gilliams's letter meshes perfectly with Pittman's letter that attempts to answer these two thorny rhetorical questions with some practical tips that nonwhite faculty can employ to protect themselves against administrative actors who may not provide the benefit of the doubt to faculty of color on campus.

Practical tips include the cautious admonition of keeping a log of all questionable interactions so that one has a record to reference in the event of future confrontations. This helpful, letter is followed by a humorous approach to interactions with tone-deaf administrators. Hernández's letter illustrates his coping mechanism for dealing with a structural system that often is quite unflinchingly stern and stoic when dealing with nonwhite faculty.

The section concludes with a captivating and cogent mentor letter, supported with examples graciously shared from his own professional life, from Harvey Charles, who wisely reminds us that collegiality in the academy does not equal equality. Dr. Charles is himself a high-level administrator, and knows firsthand how administrative conventions can both help and hinder the lives of people of color on campus. But he ends his letter by attempting to provide heart to the hopeless with prescient tips on how to successfully protect one's professional future and avoid becoming "black history."

REFERENCES

Ashraf, J. and Shabbir, T. 2006. "Are There Racial Differences in Faculty Salaries?" *Journal of Economics and Finance* 30(3): 306–16.

Chesler, M. and Young Jr., A. 2015. *Faculty Identities and the Challenge of Diversity: Reflections on Teaching in Higher Education*. New York: Routledge.

Chun, E. and Evans, A. 2012. *Diverse Administrators in Peril: The New Indentured Class in Higher Education*. Boulder, CO: Paradigm.

de Boer, F. 2015. "Why We Should Fear University, Inc.: Against the Corporate Taming of the American College." *New York Times Magazine*, September 9.

Dixon-Reeves, R. 2003. "Mentoring as a Precursor to Incorporation: An Assessment of the Mentoring Experience of Recently Minted Ph.D.s." *Journal of Black Studies* 34(1): 12–27.

González, C. 2007. "Building Sustainable Power: Latino Scholars and Academic Leadership Positions at U.S. Institutions of Higher Learning." *Journal of Hispanic Higher Education* 6(2): 157–62.

Joseph, T. and Hirshfield, L. 2011. "'Why Don't You Get Somebody New to Do It?': Race and Cultural Taxation in the Academy." *Ethnic and Racial Studies* 34(1): 121–41.

Turner, C.; González, J.; and Wood, J. 2008. "Faculty of Color in Academe: What 20 Years of Literature Tells Us." *Journal of Diversity in Higher Education* 1(3): 139–68.

U.S. Department of Education, National Center for Education Statistics. (2015). "Characteristics of Postsecondary Faculty." In *The Condition of Education 2016* (NCES 2016-144). https://nces.ed.gov/programs/coe/indicator_csc.asp.

Williams, D. A. 2007. "Achieving Inclusive Excellence: Strategies for Creating Real and Sustainable Change in Quality and Diversity." *About Campus* 12(1): 8–14.

Williams, D. and Wade-Golden, K. 2007. "The Chief Diversity Officer." *CUPA-HR Journal* 58(1): 38–48.

Chapter Eleven

Letters

LETTER 15

Dear University Hiring Committees and Administrators,

Over my years of working within the academy I have learned that dignity serves as the qualifying precursor to all that we do. Especially on university campuses, purposed with inspiring innovation and social uplift through transmitting of knowledge and creativity, dignity within the vanguard of higher education is essential. Yet, alas, I write this letter to you as a tenure-track assistant professor hoping to forestall a certain premonition of jeopardy looming over the academy as a result of the *indignation* that festers deep within the hearts and minds of faculty and staff like me: we who are intent on maintaining our dignity and the knowledge and creativity that flows from it, even while being identified as "people of color" in an academy that still feels the need to racially categorize according to American tradition.

Indignation begins early in our careers. Professionally, I can recall first sensing the mental and emotional fatigue of having to wear the white sheath over my black body, mind, and spirit while painstakingly writing (and then rewriting and reworking again) the cover letters that were to accompany my first postdoctoral job applications. The goal, of course, was to leave just enough of my identity on the page to compliment the institutions' rhetoric of appreciating diversity without raising false alarms of my being "militant" or "unconventional."

"Convention," I soon came to learn, is but one of the academy's code words for pre-*Brown v. Board of Education*–era modus operandi standards—those readily accepted by a majority European American campus. Cultural homogeneity tends to ensure comfortability. "Militant," on the other hand, is that dirty word used to target people of color, and especially African

Americans and Afro-Caribbeans, who dare to "say it loud" in public spaces, frighteningly recalling Black Power Movement-era pride. White.

For the sake of landing the job that I had earned after eleven years of secondary education, and countless sacrificed moments that might have been shared with loved ones (and, in fact, used to lessen the gap that inevitably wedges itself between the first doctor in the family and everyone else who never learned how to wear the white sheath required to fit into a "mainstream" doctoral program), I came to master the art of whittling out pieces of my authenticity with each professorate application.

Being, as my Mississippi Delta-born grandmother would say, "good at puttin' them sentences right," I mastered the self-diminishment demanded of me quickly, though not before falling flat on my honey-brown backside several times. I can recall receiving the commonly offensive "you are so articulate" during early career interviews, paired with the unmistakable look of patronizing surprise, often followed by, "We really like you Daphne, but we worry about how you might get along here since you wrote about wanting to serve your community." Or, the classic, "Do you have any other research interests than these? We don't have any faculty currently interested in these areas." Shoot. I guess I should have left that part out of my research interests.

Next time, I say to myself, I'll focus only on having a safe and ambiguous "multicultural" research agenda. Yes, that will be better: don't mention anything about racial justice, wanting to address disproportionality in special education among black children, or the need for more research into factors of resilience and hope in the inner cities. In order to exist here, I quickly learned, I must pretend that these issues are not as important to me as they really are, that these children and families are not members of my family and community; they are not people worthy of recognition and respect. My dignity has no place here.

A part of living and working in a racialized society that refuses to confront that its status as such means that research and teaching that includes non-sociopolitical-majority peoples (i.e., "people of color") becomes a specialty area rather than an integral part of intercultural university life and work. *I* become something to be parceled out. I understand very clearly now that these experiences of having been traditionally forced to the back of the room, marginalized toward having a mere shadow of presence, made visible only when it was convenient for the academy to showcase my brown face on advertisements or use my "knack" for facilitating racial diversity conversations, are caustic to me—and not only to my functioning as a professor and colleague, but also as a human being.

As professional thinkers, we know that being forced to introduce ourselves as watered-down versions of the people we are means more and lasts longer than just landing the job. It is in fact an act of self-mutilation—in this case, by the silencing of our personal voices, personalities, and professional purpose, on repeat.

First impressions have a magical way of leaving permanent marks on the memory. Having to deny our identities and inspirations at the outset of our careers in order to even be seen as a viable candidate for employment in our fields means integrating a *persona non grata* into our very professional identities. We and the search committee members who interviewed us, the administrators who decided to bet on us, and, worst of all, our students who would become the unknowing accomplices to our denied personhood all become caught in an illicit relationship, never quite legitimated by the presence of respect that comes with dignity equally shared.

So, when my comfortable and self-assured white colleague greets me today in the hallway with, "How's it going, Daphne?" with a curt smile, I suspect that what he really means is, "We're still in character, right, Daphne?" He doesn't really want to know how I'm doing with my solitary research on black children in the department, or whether I'm finding ways to settle into a secure space as an African American person at the university.

Neither he, nor anyone else born with the white privilege that precludes the need to acquire a white sheath like mine wants to "complicate" our workspace with unpleasant conversations about race or systemic racism. I get it. I smile with lips tipped with indignant knowing. "Fine, Steve, how about you?" At that self-censorship, my inspiration to think and to create wanes under a kind of spiritual persecution for an instant, or an hour; or maybe even a day. And it all began with the application process.

It is there also that the indignation can begin to subside. Thank you for reading, for change.

Sincerely,
Amanishakete Ani, Ph.D.
(Formerly called by the more "conventional" Daphne)

LETTER 16

Dear Director of the School of Social Work, (or, Racing It in Academia)
On April 27, 2012, I applied for my first teaching position in the School of Social Work. Several days later, I received an e-mail inquiring whether I was interested in teaching the Policy and Practice with Refugees course and requesting that I confirm my acceptance. I was excited when I received the news to teach the course, and wasted no time sending my response. The chances of getting a teaching position in my second year of my doctoral program seemed very unlikely but I beat the odds. Little did I know, but my first teaching experience would expose me to the stark reality of covert and

overt forms of racism from students and with no protection from administrators.

I did not know at the time that there was little to no support offered to new instructors. For example, there was no union in place, thus no collective agreement to protect the interests of instructors. There was also no formal interview for teaching positions and teaching positions were randomly assigned to students. Some students had several teaching positions while others had none. There were slim pickings for international students and students of color.

No formal training was provided prior to me assuming my new position and I was not given an opportunity to shadow a senior staff or tenured professor. No one reviewed my syllabus/course outline to ensure that it was accurate. However, to ensure my success in the position, I initiated a meeting with the professor who usually taught the course.

She was kind to share her material with me. There were no teaching workshops offered by the department. There were also no guidelines regarding my rights as an instructor or, if I encountered any concerns, no person to whom I should take them. Doctoral students were put in a position in which they would either "sink or swim." It is no wonder that some doctoral students created a pedagogy group, which served as a support system for new and current instructors. I participated in a number of these meetings and benefited from learning from other instructors. Still, this group was very homogenous and I was among only one or two persons of color who attended.

Nonetheless, I approached my first opportunity as a new adventure and was determined to do my very best in my new role. In reflecting on my teaching practice, I felt that I was very accommodating to the requests and needs of students, I checked in with them at the start of each class to address any concerns they may have had; I made myself available for in-person meetings as well as e-mail correspondence.

I had extensive discussions of assignments before and after they were marked, met with students to review assignments and provided detailed feedback and directions on how they could further improve their work. I ensured that I created a safe space in the classroom and I did my best to create an engaging and stimulating learning environment. I generated midpoint evaluations so that if issues arose, students had an opportunity to share them with me. There were no negative comments or cautionary nuances that were evident from my preliminary self-generated questionnaires. Moreover, students did not approach me with any concerns regarding my teaching or communicate that they were unhappy in the course.

Near the end of the term, students received an e-mail from the Director of the School of Social Work inviting them to complete course evaluations. These evaluations are confidential; however, quantitative results were made public. In this letter, I draw on feedback derived from the official student evaluations administered by the university, which clearly situate my experiences in the classroom as a black instructor.

The first set of student feedback depicts me as an instructor who has authority issues, challenges my presence at a prestigious university, and frames me as an awful teacher. These evaluations are a contrast to the written evaluations I had received from students in the sixth week of class. There was also no significant hostility toward me during class that would signal a major concern.

"This course has the potential to be a great course, but the instructor needs to deal with her authority issues to make the course more enjoyable."

"I find this instructor very problematic in a prestigious school like _____."

"I despised this course and regretted taking it. Patrina is patronizing, belittling, petty, and an awful teacher. Her assignments and expectations are unclear and she treated us as if we were children. I could not believe that she is actually a social worker. I am incredibly disappointed that _____ School of Social work would allow her to teach this course when she has NO EXPERIENCE WHATSOEVER WITH REFUGEES!!!"

Prior to my teaching assignment, I had previous work experience facilitating group work. I had transferable skills that I drew upon during my many interactions with students. However, I had not previously experienced such blatant and outrageous assaults in my professional practice. I wondered if students would have provided this type of feedback to a white man or woman. I also wondered how my intersecting identities of race, gender, and class influenced how students constructed me. It seemed that these impacted whether I was perceived as having integrity, being competent and credible as a black instructor.

Unlike the feedback provided by students above, which seemed more like a personal attack, this next set of student evaluations contextualizes students' experience by clearly illustrating their perceptions of factors related to instructor characteristics and teaching style, personal learning environment, and quality of teaching.

"Patrina did a great job of going over readings in class, presenting new information relating to the subject at hand, and finding ways to get class discussion going. The guest lecturers were wonderful. They gave first hand insights into social work with refugees, and really helped to expose problems they face."

"Patrina was extremely kind and welcoming to all the students. She made it evident that she valued our opinions and our learning experiences. She always encouraged class discussions and did all that she could to provide relevant information to the class. The content of the class will be valuable to me as a social worker and her approach to teaching was refreshing and appreciated."

"Ms. Patrina Duhaney, a new instructor to the School of Social Work, is a breath of fresh air. She is contemporary and approachable while being professional and excellently informed on the topic she teaches. She is willing to revise course load when as a group we advocated for some changes; this shows a great deal of maturity and flexibility lacking in other instructors at the School of Social Work."

There was much positive and valuable student feedback, however, the director of the school, at the time, focused solely on the negative feedback and used them as a gauge of my capacity as an instructor. I remembered receiving the e-mail advising me that the student evaluations had been completed and were available for me to review. There were no opportunities provided for me to meet to discuss my experiences within the classroom. As I reviewed the negative feedback, I was disheartened by the written attacks from my students. I realized just how destructive this type of feedback could be to black sessional instructors who hoped to secure future teaching opportunities.

Unfortunately, my experience is not unique. I have heard of numerous experiences in which students have berated instructors with no recourse. For example, colleagues of color have shared that students have challenged their knowledge on a particular subject; in many cases they were not viewed as legitimate bearers of knowledge, and in other cases students have ridiculed them.

I have made attempts to navigate my marginality within white institutions by involving myself as a member on student councils, participating in student groups and participating on an advisory committee for incoming and current doctoral students. However, my ability to enact change through my involvement in these groups and committees was limited. I had no voting rights at staff meetings because I was not a faculty member. The few people I could talk to who were in higher positions of power ignored or minimized the extent of the problem. Despite these challenges, I decided that I would persevere and apply for future teaching positions.

On December 20, 2013, I applied to teach six courses but was not selected to teach any of them. I did not apply for any future postings within the department mainly because I felt that I had gotten blacklisted following the negative student evaluations I had received earlier that year. Unfortunately, my early teaching experience had caused me to question my abilities and potential as an aspiring professor. I was naïve in thinking that my social location would have little bearing on my teaching experience. My sense of place in the academy quickly unraveled.

I am now sharing this with you because some time has passed since this early experience and I have had time to reflect and heal from the experience. Also, at the time of this incident, I did not believe that you were ready to hear what I had to say or willing to make changes to improve the experiences of faculty of color.

Black doctoral students who teach are marginalized and face many barriers. These students are seldom offered sessional positions and when they do, it is oftentimes after the more sought-after positions are given to white students. This unequal and unfair distribution of teaching positions is problematic in many ways.

Black women represent a small percentage of academia. Many are burdened with the added responsibility of having to carve out a place in predominantly white institutions, meeting the demands of their positions while proving they are just as good or better than their white colleagues. They are also faced with systemic racism on multiple levels.

I encourage you to hire more faculty of color, provide support for them at the onset of new teaching appointments and throughout their assignment, create mentoring opportunities for black instructors to address issues of systemic racism head-on and include input from instructors about their needs and experiences, and create an environment in which students and staff know that discrimination and racism won't be tolerated. When concerns around microaggressions, discrimination, or racism come up, create opportunities for people of color to voice their concerns and be proactive in addressing the issues.

With regards,
Patrina Duhaney

LETTER 17

Dear Lex,

I didn't believe my eyes at first. *"Temper your rhetoric"* (hooks, 1989). The last three words of the condescending presidential response to the e-mail I sent you on September 18, 2015, sent chills up my spine, confirming the challenges I negotiate as a tenured, black woman faculty member at the private, liberal arts college where we are colleagues, a college that touts itself as "a welcoming community dedicated to embracing and celebrating *all persons* from different backgrounds and cultures."

As your audacious command traveled my mind, my heart raced, jolting me into a spate of self-questioning. I bade myself to venture mentally beyond the distractions of your paternalistic sense of entitlement into my knowledge of American history, which tells the sobering truth of how fragile everything really is, how tragically committed Americans are to forgetting the racial terrain our ancestors traveled. I breathed deeply, reminding myself of the politics of responsibility that is my work.

In the initial e-mail I sent, I had asked you to conduct an investigation into the disturbing matter of a first-year, black male student's having been banned from one of the residence halls for arguing with—not threatening, harming, or violating—a white woman student who dared him to "go and get his *black* girlfriends," given his insistence that she lower the noise in her room, which was disturbing his sick friend's attempt to rest. I explained to you that the student, only several weeks into his first semester at the college, sought me out though I'd never met or taught him previously, sharing with me the details of his encounters with several Public Safety officers and Residence Life staff, mainly because doing so allowed him the safe, cultural space to give voice to the dispiriting and demoralizing encounters he endured in the presence of "authority." He had also heard through the grapevine that in addition to being one of only three black faculty members here, I am intentional about supporting and speaking up for black students on campus.

Many of the students who seek me out want to speak and truly be heard, affirmed, valued, and reminded of their need to persevere in the face of the daily racial microaggressions (everyday slights, insults, and indignities [real or imagined; intentional or not] directed toward one racial/ethnic group by another group or by structural/institutional whiteness) that undermine their hopes and dreams.

They also want to know how I manage to persevere, how I maintain my dignity and stay true to my ideals. There are no simple answers to their questions; however, I almost always tell them that my work at Albright is bigger than my professional obligations to the college. It is both my honor and duty to continue the work of my ancestors, using my privilege and abilities to help restore what slavery denied black people.

Last spring, the president of the Xion Step Team, a senior student, notified me of my need, as faculty adviser, to be present for the duration of the organization's spring party, which was scheduled on a Friday night from 9:30 p.m. to 1 a.m. I always attend the step show, but my suddenly being "required" to attend the after-party did not sit well with me for a number of reasons, the main one being the discriminatory practice informing the requirement. She had explained that the organization wouldn't be allowed to have the party unless I attended.

To be sure that I wasn't misreading the new rule, I conducted an informal poll of my colleagues across campus who also advise student organizations. Not a single one knew anything about this policy. Worse yet, they were dumbfounded when I asked whether they observed anyone being wanded by Public Safety officers at any campus events. I shuddered as I heard myself describing the required police presence at the Xion campus parties where a minimum of four public safety officers, after being paid from the students' organizational budget, electronically wand entering guests and then circulate during the party, standing on the dance floor, giving stern looks to the party-goers, signaling their authority and power should misconduct arise.

When I presented this issue last spring at a Campus Life Council meeting where the Dean of Students was present, calling a foul on the overt discrimination that our black students face when such policies are enacted, she got defensive but took no responsibility. Did she apprise you of this matter? I ask because I'm trying to determine whether your reply grew from a place of unknowing or complicity. If it's unknowing, let me clarify my aim. I situated myself firmly between students of color and your administration because we live in a world where black lives are systematically and intentionally targeted for destruction. These students' matriculation at a majority white institution doesn't alter that reality. Furthermore, their stories of wanting to be treated fairly and with respect on and beyond campus are narratives I listen to regularly.

I asked you to examine the direct correlation between the black male student's incident and the racial profiling and over-policing that occurred during the Xion party. I asked, too, that you initiate implementation of practices and policies that hold members of our institution accountable for denying fair treatment to all of our students. You offered the following response:

> I agree that the student's narrative is disturbing, but it's also disturbing that you appear ready to assume misconduct on the part of our student life staff without any further evidence or testimony. It looks uncomfortably like what you are accusing them of in their treatment of [student's name withheld]. Not terribly helpful, collegial, or professional. I can assure you that we'll take your concerns seriously, but you'd be more likely to get better results if you could find a way to *temper your rhetoric*.

I did not find your perception of me as causing problems all by myself surprising, mainly because I recalled your similar response several years ago during a meeting of the Strategic Planning Committee in which I challenged your inflexible model of governance and simultaneous dismissal of the committee's hard work because it did not meet your standards or approval. That time you thanked me for my "evangelical" comments. This time you suggest that I "temper my rhetoric." Implicit in both responses was your insensitivity to and rejection of ideas or positions different from yours. What struck me most about the language you used was your attempt to exert power, perhaps to be seen as the definer of my reality.

In light of Nietzsche's contention in *On the Genealogy of Morals* that "a strong and well-constituted [wo]man digests h[er] experiences (deeds and misdeeds all included) as [s]he digests h[er] meals, even when [s]he has to swallow some tough morsels" (Nietzsche), I replied to your e-mail explaining that I would temper my rhetoric when the same consideration and treatment given to the white female student is extended to the black male student who was banned from the residence hall. I also suggested that you avoid telling me how to feel about racism and sexism and how to express those feelings as they relate to our black students' racially charged campus experiences.

Finally, I qualified my belief that my past efforts at trying to work through the biases that rear their ugly heads every year have been neither effective nor fair to our students who endure ongoing feelings of alienation. I asked you to consider talking to them so that you can hear their narratives firsthand and respond in real time. You never replied. Rather than interpret your silence, thereby widening the wedge that currently exists between us, I invite you, as Audre Lorde advised, to transform your silence "into language and action [a]s an act of self-revelation." ("The Transformation of Your Silence into Language and Action" is a speech by Audre Lorde that was originally delivered at the Lesbian and Literature panel of the Modern Language Association's December 28, 1977 meeting.)

I wasn't seeking your comradeship or approval when I reached out to you. I wanted *you* to look at the black students at the college as an important part of the whole community, admit that the systems (as they now function) are broken, and take some responsibility for the problem. I wanted to trust that you could help facilitate a long-overdue critique of the broken system and prioritize a plan of action to dismantle systemic institutional discrimination college-wide. Above all, I expected you to care, to show compassion and concern. Instead, you scorned and declared my insistence on racial justice to be merely rhetorical while simultaneously choosing to be blind to injustice and the suffering of a black student.

From where I stand, there is a fundamental disconnect between the world in which you function as a white, male college president in the 21st century and the reality facing a large number of the black students you claim to champion. By contributing to the disempowerment of the black community at the college, not only by attempting to chastise and silence me, but also by communicating the message that the white patriarchal order maintains control of the narratives of all Others, you showed yourself to be a leader in need of a radical reconsideration of priorities, strategies, messages, and staffing that replace the outdated paradigm informing the college's structural arrangements, practices, and policies. The fierce urgency of now, as Martin Luther King Jr. once called it, requires that I challenge you to heed James Baldwin's prophetic charge to "cease fleeing from reality and begin to change it" (Baldwin, 1962, 10).

Signed,
Dr. Teresa Gilliams

REFERENCES

Baldwin, J. 1962. *The Fire Next Time*. New York: Vintage, 1993: 5–10.
hooks, B. 1989. *Talking Back: Thinking Feminist, Thinking Black*. Boston: South End, 12.
Nietzsche, F. *On the Genealogy of Morals*, Essay 3, Aphorism 16.

LETTER 18

Dear Unsupported Faculty "Teaching in Color,"

Raced and gendered oppression have long been evident in my classroom experiences, student teaching evaluations, and review processes. I've sought informal and formal support to address them, but my university was not equipped (nor willing?) to support faculty of color navigating the classroom.

Nonetheless, I earned a successful review. Hooray, right? No. The official letter congratulated me for the accomplishment, then one sentence stated that without improvement in my student teaching evaluations my review the following year would be unsuccessful. Wait . . . what? I was stunned by the threat and its lack of detail or depth.

To sort out the threat, a mentor suggested I ask the following: (1) Which items did they want improved?; (2) How did they define "improvement"?; and (3) Where were their suggestions and support toward that improvement? I requested this information informally but was referred to the high-level administrator who oversaw the review. My meeting request expressed a commitment to the university and thus a desire to know how I could improve my teaching evaluations. Here are the highlights of that meeting:

Before I could utter one word, I was aggressively told that racism did not exist on our campus.

"Dr. X" was suggested as my teaching mentor. I politely mentioned I'd had a "difficult" interaction with Dr. X. I was swiftly scolded and told that Dr. X was not racist. I had not mentioned nor even implied racism but, indeed, Dr. X—one of the most powerful faculty on campus—had a notorious reputation as a racist.

I was informed that due to my "young" (30–40 years old) age, I did not know what racism looked like and was mistaken if I thought I'd ever experienced it on campus. I was advised that in the unlikely event that I should experience racism on campus, I should brush it off instead of taking it "personally."

Finally, I was bluntly told that the real issue was beyond my teaching evaluations because faculty didn't like the "tone" of my review materials and the "way I held my head" around campus. The confusion obviously worn on my face was dissolved when the administrator offered the clarification that I was an "uppity black woman."

I was numb both during and after this meeting. I felt as though I'd been repeatedly punched in the gut with invalidations of the raced experiences I hadn't even mentioned and aggressive admonitions to back me down from even thinking about mentioning them. Further, I suffered a slap in the face from the bold declaration that the threat to my upcoming review was because I'd somehow stepped outside the boundaries afforded to black women.

I immediately informed several high-level administrators about this racist and sexist meeting. None of them denied that it had happened, yet none of them used their institutional power to address or mitigate its implications for my review. Nothing happened. At all. This incident crystallized my belief that faculty of color must support and protect themselves regarding teaching issues. Below I describe the strategies I both personally use and suggest to others navigating being a person of color in the classroom. Perhaps some or all of these strategies can help you survive and thrive if you find yourself in a similar unsupportive situation for your "Teaching in Color."

The most important fact I had to learn and also want you to know is this: It is not *you* nor your "fault." Research on classroom experiences, student evaluations, and personnel reviews of teaching demonstrate that racial oppression is common in faculty of color's teaching experiences. Remember, not you, not you, OK? Not you. Racism is not your fault. But there are things you can do to protect yourself and deal with these experiences as you come across them.

Provide Research on Faculty of Color's Teaching Experiences to Others

I did and encourage others to take advantage of and create opportunities to share research on faculty of color's teaching experience to allies, chairs, provosts, and so forth. It becomes another narrative that makes it clear that negative treatment experiences are not about you or your teaching. Both anecdotal and research evidence suggests that negative course evaluations and negative student classroom behavior are unfortunate but common experiences for faculty of color. Be mindful that you can also reference this research evidence in your promotion and tenure review material. When you share these materials, you focus the narrative on race in the classroom versus you as a deficient teacher.

Practice a Daily Teaching Coping Strategy

Develop a daily teaching ritual or coping strategy. Perhaps you have teaching theme music that you play as you head into campus or once you're already in your office. Choose music that fits whatever you need: peace of mind, balance, humor, hype music, and so forth. For years, my teaching theme music has been DMX's "Party Up (Up In Here)": "Ya'll Gon' Make Me Lose My

Mind, Up in Here, Up in Here!" It provided the acknowledgment of the crazy and high energy I needed to face whatever awaited me in the classroom.

Choose an end of day teaching ritual. My personal favorites are to enjoy a bike ride or movie after I finish teaching. It's a way to signal that teaching is over and that it is now time to focus my energy on something else and often something restorative. And of course, meet with a therapist about teaching stress if your coping strategies do not work.

Identify or Develop a Teaching Community

Identify or develop a teaching community where you can discuss classroom experiences. I am grateful to have had such a community for years. This group must be comprised of individuals with whom you share similar teaching priorities (e.g., time spent, work-life balance, pedagogy, etc.). The community's purpose is to provide a safe space where you can vent and strategize about your teaching. Check in with it on a regular basis to keep you from bottling up your emotions and proactive in relation to your teaching experiences.

Use Student-Centered Practices to Focus Students on the Course Content

Student-centered practices are proven as effective at increasing both content knowledge and skills. This style of teaching also takes you and your race and gender identities out of the center of the classroom. So instead of being the sage on the stage, you become the person of color on the stage or the woman on the stage and some students may not be able to get past that. Teaching with student-centered strategies (e.g., discussions, debates, group work) requires that students are actively involved in the learning process versus focusing on you as the "inadequate" deliverer of a lecture.

To be clear, I am not suggesting that you relinquish your legitimate authority or expertise in the classroom. Instead I am highlighting successful teaching strategies that keep students focused on learning and thereby reduces the ability/time/energy they have to focus on *you*.

Reduce Time Spent on Teaching

I initially reacted to negative and mixed student evaluations by spending an inordinate time on teaching preparation. Over-preparation is a common response to anxiety about the classroom or teaching evaluations. You try to cover too much material, spend inordinate time writing lectures or designing teaching activities. There are too many ideas for you to cover in the allotted time and students can't keep up with what you're teaching.

Over-prepping attempts to convince students we are legitimate, to reduce feelings of imposter syndrome, to eliminate the space students have to enact racially oppressive behaviors, and so forth. Unfortunately, it cannot guarantee any of these outcomes and oftentimes results in little time left for anything else. You cannot control how students interact with you but you CAN control how you respond. For these reasons, the best way to deal with raced teaching experiences is to identify and enact ways to reduce the time you spent on teaching and increase time for other activities (e.g., research, family).

Again, I want to reiterate: It's not you. No amount of good behavior on your part is going to overcome racism. Your teaching is not the cause of raced teaching evaluations or classroom incivility. While no one's teaching is perfect, nothing is inherently "wrong" with your teaching when compared to the average colleague's teaching quality. I emphasize this because faculty of color should not invest huge amounts of time and energy to "fix" their teaching.

That said, crazy teaching situations may arise that you then will have to deal with and address. While I always push for institutional change to better support faculty of color (and encourage others to do the same), that support may not occur in a timely manner if at all for you. So I urge you to use the above-suggested strategies to navigate, persist, and thrive as a person of color in the classroom.

All the best,
Chavella Pittman

LETTER 19

Dear Chief Diversity Officers: Pedigree or Ph.D.? (or, "You Can't Handle the Truth")

So, the story goes like this: I was meeting the Dean of Faculty at a small liberal arts college (but not the one I am currently at). The dean, charming as they all seem to be, was kindly asking where I was from. "I'm from a Southern California town called Whittier," I say. "You may know it as the place where Richard Nixon is from," "That's right," the dean said. "It's also where Whittier College is located." "Why yes, my mother used to work at the college," I shared. "Really?" the dean asked. "In what department?"

And then I replied . . . drumroll please . . . , "The cafeteria."

We both smiled slyly. I may have even apologized for the seemingly set-up nature of this joke. But it wasn't a joke. It's the truth. It's part of my background, plain and simple. It's just that in certain contexts, my pedigree is an odd fit, often humorous, often humiliating, especially in this particular industry, the academy.

As faculty of color, we are often asked where we're from, or, where we're *really* from. These queries can be well-intentioned, aggressively probing, or just small talk. Sharing these histories with colleagues is the risky part, and can be fraught with discomfort.

The fact of the matter is that our histories—my history—can easily overshadow my resume or trump my sense of belonging in this profession to which I've dedicated many years. For me, this is an uncomfortable, ongoing feeling.

I'm Mexican. I grew up poor, on food stamps, raised by a single mother. We didn't have Christmas trees, vacations, summer camps, or birthday parties. I also went to a Catholic school, have a complicated relationship with the Spanish language, and I am a first-generation college student—and a first-generation lots-of-things, for that matter. Is this what people want to know?

How about another story? One time, while a tenure-track faculty member at a Research One institution, I was at a barbecue with senior colleagues from a different department than my own. But that fact wouldn't matter much. Anyway, we were talking about drinking and dive bars (and we were all doing a little drinking, too). As we chatted about bars, I volunteered that I had "grown up in a bar." I wasn't actually raised in a bar, but as a child, if I wanted to visit my Dad, the T&L Tavern was the place where I had to go. Weekends, holidays, school days, birthdays: I spent a lot of time there. My two brothers, one older and one younger, became experts at shooting pool as a result. I was more into the jukebox, the peanuts, the beef jerky.

None of my colleagues, however, heard this slightly longer explanation, because the statement that "I grew up in a bar" finished the conversation. People went silent, excused themselves. Some stared at the ground. As it turns out, not all colleagues shared in the laugh the way the dean had. Instead, there was silence. Crickets. No one said a word, unless projecting pity is a form of speech. Of course, I felt more than silence. I knew that I had shared too much history. This time, this story, would not go over as humor, or some interesting fact of my background.

What I have learned from these experiences is that my biography can define me more powerfully than my scholarly record. It's often pedigree that matters more than a Ph.D. The doctorate doesn't level the playing the field. In fact, it opens you up to further scrutiny. People will reach into your history to find what's missing, what's different, what's not normal, and what is not normative.

So, for me, telling my history brings a lot of this back. It's not that I have any shame for this time period. Quite the opposite. I have hilarious stories of growing up, wrestling with difference, but sometimes they come back to haunt me, to define me, because other people can't handle it, cannot see past my background and how it fits or doesn't fit into the academy. For many people (and not just people of color, but many "others") we are mostly defined from the outside. We are so often judged by our biographies.

I have an additional point about biography—about history—that I think is lacking from many institutional conversations about "diversity." Although, for many of us, history hangs like an albatross, as a punishment, it's the very thing that's missing from discussions of diversity. Usually, we get hung up on the "diversity is good" mantra. "Diversity as a goal." Intentional diversity, affirmative diversity, et cetera, et cetera. But the part of "diversity" that doesn't get talked about is actually its history, its particular biography, where it's *really from*.

Many of the mechanisms intended to promote diversity, especially in higher education, were originally meant to remedy the historical, systematic, and cruel inequalities suffered by the usual subjects: poor people, women, gays and lesbians, individuals with disabilities, trans-persons, people of color, and those who are combinations of many of these. History has done a number on these communities—one that has lasted—and promoted the accumulation of wealth, power, and privilege for others. Mechanisms of diversity used to take into account the uneven playing field, the generations of exclusion, the persistent danger or silence around nonnormative "diverse" qualities. But that's gone now, perhaps forgotten.

Whether you talk about the remnants of affirmative action policies, color blindness, or the "diversity is good" model, all of these presume a level playing field. All of these forget history. They hang their hats on the value added by diversity (or in contrast, some people also discuss the "costs" of diversity). Diversity undoubtedly has value, is worth adding, but it's also steeped in history and has its own critical past.

So we have a contradiction here. On one hand, many of us are persistently defined by our biographies—we can't control this dialogue—but it's actually history that's been eviscerated from the hard work, processes, and mechanisms of "diversity and inclusion" that many have long forgotten.

Sincerely,
David Hernández

Chapter Twelve

Mentor Essay

Reflections on Higher Ed Administration

Harvey Charles, University of Albany

I have spent my entire professional career in higher education, and after 25 years as an administrator, conclude that I have been fortunate to work on college and university campuses. I have heard horror stories about life in private industry, or even in the federal government, and think that I've been shielded from many of the difficulties that plague those institutions. But life can be hell in higher education, as many of the letters in this volume attest.

It is a place reputed to be awash with liberals who supposedly value principles of equality and diversity. It is therefore often shocking for young faculty of color like you to discover powerful hierarchies in a place that preaches collegiality and to discover multiple forms of racist behavior committed by many who publicly advocate for diversity. The contradictions and hypocrisies can be overwhelming!

The tragic reality about racism in America is that it is so pervasive that few places are safe from its reach. Even the power that having a budget and a senior administrative title confers is not enough to shield one from these challenges. As an administrator, I have gained a perspective that most faculty rarely have. It is from this vantage point that I wish to offer some insights that can help you steer clear of the land mines and read the code in which racism is often masked.

UNDERSTANDING THAT COLLEGIALITY DOESN'T MEAN EQUALITY

I like to say that the faces may differ, but the issues and the personalities tend to be the same, regardless of the institution. In this regard, one can usually find a few faculty members who relish the role of being a thorn in the side of the administration at practically every college or university. They generally receive positive strokes from their colleagues for playing this role, and from time to time, can be quite effective at rallying other faculty members to a particular cause that, at its core, either condemns an administrative decision or calls the administration to account.

I have seen younger, untenured faculty members manipulated by older tenured faculty members to be the front person for these kinds of causes, calling out the administration on one issue or another. For untenured faculty members, this is always a risky role to play and for faculty of color, it can be practically a death wish in terms of long-term viability at the institution. In the short term, you may win brownie points among your colleagues for what they may regard as your courage and the principled stances you take, but in the long term, you may be hung out to dry.

Like most humans, administrators don't like to be made to look bad, they don't like to be accused of acting in bad faith and they don't like to be humiliated in public. Get on their bad sides, and you may find your request for funding for a very worthy project has been turned down by the dean. Challenge them, and you may find that the provost didn't consider you for a plum administrative opening for which you are very qualified. Rub them the wrong way, and you may live to endure the worst outcome of all, denial of tenure—not necessarily by your faculty colleagues, but by the provost or the president who may be acting unilaterally or at the behest of the Board of Trustees. This is not being said to suggest that you should never complain or raise questions when they are due, but when you do, it is important to keep in mind the following:

- that your voice may be much more diminished than you think simply because you are a person of color, regardless of the support that may be coming from some of your white colleagues;
- that there may be adverse consequences simply for speaking up; and
- that pushing back against a practice or policy can be done without character assassination, demeaning accusations, or overt hostility.

IN THE END, RACIAL/ETHNIC IDENTITY ALWAYS MATTERS — TO THEM

I have long come to disabuse myself of the politics of respectability. Racism in the United States makes it impossible for race to go unnoticed, regardless of how much liberals talk about color blindness, and regardless of the accomplishments of people of color. I remember cochairing an important committee with a long-standing full professor who also happened to chair the search committee that hired me. I wrote the final report of this committee because I was most knowledgeable about the deliberations of the various subcommittees, and I figured that it would be the most efficient way to complete the report, giving the cochair an opportunity to modify the draft as he saw fit before its dissemination.

Upon receiving the draft report, he expressed surprise, bordering on amazement, at how extremely well-written the report was, and then in a moment of unsolicited honesty, proceeded to tell me how he was initially concerned about my ability to do the job when I was first hired, but with the passage of time, realized that I was succeeding just fine. I was recruited by a search firm for this position, which meant that I had to be a compelling candidate for them to recommend me.

I had very strong credentials, both in terms of my academic training/ professional accomplishments and even relative to the other finalists. The chair, by virtue of his role, was more knowledgeable than most about the details of all three finalists. And yet, he was surprised at my writing skills and initially doubtful that I could do the job I had been doing for the past twelve years. In thinking that he was offering me a compliment, he unwittingly revealed a racist perspective on my abilities, a pattern that professionals of color still encounter far too often.

The moral of this story is that you should never be seduced by the idea that because you earned your degree at a prestigious institution or were trained by one of the preeminent scholars in your field, that your race has become a nonissue. Even if your work is viewed through the lens of pedigree, it is equally likely that it will be evaluated through the lens of race or gender.

It is for this reason that if seven peer-reviewed articles published in top journals are required for tenure, you should have eight or nine or ten to put on the table. And if you can add a book to this body of work, as well as important service work, so much the better. And while having gone over and above to meet the stated standards does not guarantee tenure, it effectively removes a reason that can be cited for denial.

Having said this, one African American colleague whose portfolio exceeded the stated expectations for tenure in terms of research, teaching, and service was challenged by her white colleagues about the student evaluations she received, which were the highest earned by any professor in that particular department. In their minds, these results were suspect because it was unacceptable to not identify at least one "flaw" in her profile, whether contrived or not, as she moved toward a positive tenure decision.

Remember that your best job is not the one you have, but the one to which you are going. And in this regard, embrace the idea that you may need to move on from your current institution. Mobility isn't a bad thing, even for tenured faculty, and with a strong portfolio, you should be able to generate interest elsewhere.

UNDERSTAND THE POLITICAL NATURE OF TENURE

I am often struck by how little new faculty understand about how the academy, and tenure in particular, works. The granting of tenure is a political process: it always has been and probably always will be, and the United States is filled with examples of tenure gained and tenure denied that confirms this view. I can think of two cases, both at the same institution, where tenure was awarded even though these individuals did not meet the minimum standards set in terms of publications. (Note that the ostensibly secretive nature of the deliberations made no difference to those who wanted to know and on a campus like this, there were no real secrets.)

As to why this happened? Well, these individuals were well-liked by their colleagues, and, with a wink and a nod, a way just had to be found to keep them on. Two men of color turned out to not be as fortunate, however. One exceeded the standards for tenure and had won acclaim in his field that no one else in the department had enjoyed. His failing? He was not sufficiently subservient to the power brokers in his department. He didn't show up to all departmental meetings; he wasn't friends with the chair. He became black history!

The political nature of tenure means that in order to successfully navigate this process, you, too, must be political. The first order of business, of course, is to follow the requirements to the letter and then some, exceeding the stated requirements as much as you can. This will come in handy if tenure is denied and you decide to sue or to go on the job market.

The second is to cultivate allies both within and outside of your department, and consult with a senior faculty you trust to help you figure out how to negotiate the difficult situations that will inevitably arise. Project the image of someone who is a team player, and while this does not mean doing *everything* you are asked to do, do your part and ensure that it is sufficiently visible so that others know that you are making a contribution. Attend social gatherings, and even if it may gross you out to socialize with people you view as phony or even racists, it's about playing the game. It doesn't mean that you get drunk with these people or invite them on vacation. You can show up, circulate a bit, and then slip out.

ALIGN YOUR WORK WITH INSTITUTIONAL PRIORITIES IN VISIBLE WAYS

Find a way to align the work you do as a faculty member with one or more of the priorities articulated by the president and/or provost. For example, retention is now a hot topic on campuses across the United States, particularly at institutions where state appropriations are tied to this metric. Might you be able to institute strategies in your facilitation of learning experiences with students that can demonstrate that it serves the goal of retention?

On other campuses, blended learning has become a huge priority. It might be wise to use this approach in some of the courses you teach. Applied learning or curriculum internationalization may be institutional priorities where you are based. It may not take much to adopt these priorities in your work. Indeed, you may already have incorporated these principles in your work but never described them as such.

In short, there may be many "low-hanging fruit" that can be harvested to demonstrate that you have intentionally aligned your work with the priorities of the administration and for this, you may earn many brownie points. This is also a way of making yourself *appear* to be indispensable. While is it true that no one is indispensable, particularly in an era where tenure-track positions are scarce and lecturers (in most disciplines) are available a dime a dozen, administrators hate to lose faculty who are getting grants, are loved by students, and are making an impact on their discipline and department.

SEEK ALLIES AMONG ADMINISTRATORS/FACULTY WHO ARE PEOPLE OF COLOR

As resources to support faculty become more challenging to access, it is wise to get to know and support administrators who have an interest in the work you do. For example, the Vice President for Student Affairs may be interested in your psychology class's project that looks at the reported experience of campus life between those who have meals at the campus cafeteria regularly and those who do not.

This administrator may be willing to pay the cost of student or faculty travel to a conference to present the findings of this study if the findings would be shared with her as well. The Associate Provost for Applied Learning may provide you with research support if you were to introduce him to the small business owners who attend your on-campus workshops. These individuals may represent opportunities for internship placement in the local community and therefore help the Associate Provost create additional opportunities for students.

Be aware, however, that these alliances may attract the attention of others in ways that may not always be flattering. I recall taking a group of science faculty to Australia and New Zealand to visit colleagues at our partner universities, but with the unstated goal of helping to convince them of the value of study abroad. The following year, with the approval of the provost, I took an interdisciplinary group of faculty to southern Africa; they were all either teaching courses on Africa or the African American experience, but had never been to Africa themselves.

I viewed this trip as necessary to help them further globalize their pedagogy and also help launch study abroad experiences to Africa that they would lead. Although nothing happened when the science faculty returned to campus, there was an uproar when the faculty who travelled to southern Africa returned. How could I decide to take a group of faculty to Africa? Was this an appropriate way to spend college resources? How come one other faculty member who taught courses on Africa did not go?

The indictment was that I did not follow "process," that seemingly neutral term that gets trotted out when the gatekeepers aren't happy with an issue. Yet, not one of the individuals who viewed my trip as problematic had had any issue with the science faculty traveling to Australia and New Zealand the previous year, although the same "process" had been followed. Well, it turns out that the latter group consisted of all white faculty.

The faculty members who travelled to Africa were all black. In effect, the message was this: how dare the black man (forget my administrative title) take a group of black faculty to Africa (or anywhere for that matter) without the consultation and approval of those who believed it was their right to give. For this, I was marked as having too much autonomy and attempts were made to rein me in.

To add insult to injury, the provost made sympathetic nods to the complainers as if to suggest that I had not acted properly in securing institutional approval for this trip. Thankfully, the faculty found this trip enormously rewarding and a number of them maintained ties and launched programs in Africa that continued years after that trip ended. The importance of creating allies among administrators and among colleagues who are people of color cannot be overstated. They may be the only people to whom you can turn in the face of difficulties.

A young faculty member of color who was recruited at an institution where I was based soon ran into turbulence with the senior faculty member who recruited her because she resisted his instructions about how she should teach a particular course. This was after she had accepted a heavier teaching load than any other junior or senior professor was given and had acted like a team player in every other way.

To further punish the junior faculty, a course for which she had the greatest amount of expertise in the department was assigned to an adjunct faculty with marginal expertise, and she was made to teach low-level general education courses. The straw that broke the camel's back was when she was threatened with never again being able to find a position within the field, and discovering to her dismay, that search committees for positions to which she had applied at other universities stopped reviewing her application because they had been surreptitiously contacted by this senior faculty member to discourage them from considering her candidacy.

In effect, the senior faculty member was not only determined to make her life hell in the department, but was also determined to block her efforts at finding alternative employment at other institutions. What was pretty stunning was that other faculty in the department closed ranks behind the senior faculty member who was perpetuating this despicable behavior. Thankfully, I along with a couple other senior faculty of color were able to advocate for a switch in academic departments for this junior faculty and she was able to continue her career without the trauma of dealing with what had become a hostile workplace.

CONCLUSION

If you think the academy is bad, be assured that life isn't necessarily better outside of it. Racism is a fact of life in America and it is well ensconced in the academy. It is possible, however, to survive and even thrive in the academy. It is possible to inspire students to realize new pathways of thinking, to push the boundaries of knowledge with your scholarship, and to transform the academy into an exciting and stimulating community because of the unique experiences you bring as a person of color. If you want to be in the academy and you have prepared yourself for such a career, then you must claim your right to be there and defend your ground with courage and with the support of those who care about your success.

V

Climate

Chapter Thirteen

Major Themes in the Research on Faculty of Color and Campus Climate

The orchestrated, politically mandated nature of the interview and hiring process creates campus climates and institutions that faculty of color are more likely to perceive as unsupportive, non-collegial, and unfriendly (Thomas and Hollenshead, 2001). In these climates, they negotiate accusations of tokenism among predominantly white faculty. The culture of tokenism is such that faculty of color who are few in number at their universities feel that they have to be twice as good as their white colleagues in order to gain recognition for their efforts and have to negotiate the isolation of "being the only one" in fields that thrive on collaborative research, teaching, and service environments.

Because faculty of color are one of few, they are stretched in many different directions by administrators who want them to be "racial representatives" based on their racial identity and/or their scholarship. These institutional conditions mean that faculty of color are subject to high levels of cultural taxation, stress, and sometimes, burnout (Stanley, 2006; Turner et al., 2008).

The campus climate is one that is fraught with racially forged tensions between white students, faculty and staff, and students of color. The fact is that colleges and universities in the United States were built to cater to affluent, white, American men. As the national context has transformed through social movements for women's rights, the liberation of people of color, working class and immigrant inclusion, increased religious freedom, and LGBT visibility, the university has become a battleground for the beginnings or the extensions of these revolutions. As a result, faculty of color are hired into deeply politically contentious institutional environments where marginalized students, faculty, and staff are vying for position in socially exclusive institutions.

More recently, the Black Lives Matter movement, which started as a response to police brutality in black communities, has transformed into a contemporary civil rights struggle where preexisting contentious politics of race, class, gender, and sexuality have entered university classrooms, residential halls, and public spaces. Because college campuses are increasingly racially heterogeneous spaces where whites may reproduce their privilege, the cultural belonging of students and faculty of color who share the same spaces are compromised. From these realities emerge deep conflicts.

University public relations campaigns then seek to quiet students of color and their white allies who live and learn in unequal academic and residential structures. As campuses where diverse groups of students, faculty, and staff come together in the name of consuming and producing knowledge, campuses are mini–social worlds with their own hierarchical systems and tense power relations. As a result, faculty of color often find themselves negotiating their own power in this space, but also using whatever power they have to improve their students' experience on campus.

Few faculty of color seem to be able to find a balance between self-preservation and community involvement. They often either withdraw from campus culture altogether or, in fully engaging with the social problems they and their students and colleagues experience, eventually compromise their long-term professional productivity and well-being.

When faculty of color walk into the often exclusionary spaces of their classrooms, offices, and faculty meetings, they have to assert their power and position more blatantly than their white peers, whose status in a white-dominant hegemony is literally written on their bodies. The cultural mismatch in styles of speech, dress, and expression between faculty of color and their white colleagues, administrators, and students means that they have to find innovative ways to display contributions to the university space without stepping on any land mines. Because campus climates are inherently stressful and conflicted, faculty of color are also balancing universities that are deeply invested in capitalistic logics more than the actual development of their students and faculty.

We have seen this in many cases, such as the University of Missouri's controversy around white faculty and administrators who ignore the hostile antiblack environments that their students have to live and learn in until their economic engine, football, is threatened. Therefore, faculty of color seek limited support systems to address their students' grievances and problems, while their own problems within the same institution are abundant, and experienced daily. This process is fraught with uncertainty, particularly since offices of Equal Opportunity and Human Resources on campus are either ill-equipped or don't have the political will to transform the institutional inadequacies and individual biases that too often plague campuses.

The essays in this section reflect on the myriad challenges that exist on campus and how faculty of color navigate them. Jamil's letter highlights the ways in which knowledge production on college campuses continues to privilege the ideas and contributions of white scholars over nonwhite scholars. Jamil provides a vivid description of the ways in which whiteness privileges white scholars' perspectives on Muslim "others" over Muslim academics themselves. This letter compels us to consider the intersection of race, religion, and gender in how faculty of color are treated in academic circles. In particular, when faculty of color conduct research on minority populations, the campus climate is such that their opinions are marginalized, discredited, or considered what many call "me-search," a pejorative term used by white academics to describe the connectedness between one's identity and their scholarship.

Similar to Jamil's letter, Jones's letter demarcates the contradictory hypervisibility yet invisibility that faculty of color experience on their college campuses. In the post–Civil Rights era, the diversification of college campuses recreates what Jones describes as a hierarchy of first-, second-, and third-class citizens of that space. She outlines the enormous intellectual and emotional labor she endures and the "survival strategies" used in order to assert her space in a university system where she is rendered an outsider on the basis of her race, class, gender, and sexuality.

Davis's letter to junior faculty of color who are in the early days of their membership in the "club" recounts jarring encounters with misrecognition and racism from white colleagues. She shares her strategy of survival, called "strategic positioning." Strategic positioning encourages new faculty of color to assess their agendas as either conventional or trailblazing scholars, and to cultivate identities and practices that align with their goals.

While the Jones piece provides junior faculty of color with a long view of what to expect from the culture of academia during their journey to tenure, Hunter's letter is a retrospective piece on the numerous lessons on racism she has learned in her 30 years as a professor in a predominately white institution. She reflects on the nature of racism as a "respecter of no one," requiring repetition and mindfulness in order to exist on white, liberal college campuses.

The mentor essay by sociologist Eduardo Bonilla-Silva ties together this section by providing numerous prescriptions for graduate students and faculty of color who operate daily in academic institutions founded on American iterations of global whiteness, domination, and power. In order to outline the toxicity of culture on historically white university campuses, he recounts his own struggles as an AmeRícan, from his time as a graduate student to his current status as an accomplished scholar.

On the one hand, he ably demonstrates its structural inevitability, but on the other, he also frames the role of white power in the construction of the university system and reminds us that the culture that ties together the university business of teaching, research, and service flows from reproducing the white status quo. With this awareness, faculty of color are encouraged to stay the course, and disrupt this process through their continued presence, survival, and success.

REFERENCES

Stanley, C. 2006. "Coloring the Academic Landscape: Faculty of Color Breaking the Silence in Predominantly White Colleges and Universities." *American Educational Research Journal* 43(4): 701–36.

Thomas, G. D. and Hollenshead, C. 2001. "Resisting from the Margins: The Coping Strategies of Black Women and Other Women of Color Faculty Members at a Research University." *Journal of Negro Education* 70(3); 166–75.

Turner, C.; González, J.; and Wood, J. 2008. "Faculty of Color in Academe: What 20 Years of Literature Tells Us." *Journal of Diversity in Higher Education* 1(3): 139–68.

Chapter Fourteen

Letters

Dear Director, (or, Good Muslims and White Academics)

I am writing to share with you something that happened last year when you invited a series of guest speakers to this university. One of them was a European academic. You didn't attend his lecture, but I did.

His topic was the integration of Muslims in Europe. What he said was generally the mainstream discourse about Muslim minorities in Western societies: that Muslims need to demonstrate that they are "good citizens" of Europe by integrating. By integration, he meant that they should be "good Muslims," follow the laws of the country they live in, learn more about its history and try to "tone down" their "visibility" as Muslims through clothing, mosques, and other "demands" because it created negative feelings and relations with non-Muslims. He gave examples from several European countries.

Though I disagreed with what he said, what struck me the most was that in that 45-minute lecture, he looked primarily at and spoke to the white people in the room. I was sitting directly in his line of sight across the room, yet he looked at the white male academic sitting next to me. It was a small audience, probably about 12 people. It included other academic research staff from our department, all of them people of color, whom he had already met before his lecture. I was sitting near them, and I was one of two Muslim scholars of color present. There were also a few white academics from other departments of the university.

I was the first person to raise my hand for the Q & A. I wanted to see if he would look at me when I spoke to him. Would he acknowledge my presence—a brown, Muslim, female presence sitting in his line of sight directly across the room from him?

I made several points: that laws are not neutral, that current antiterrorism laws operate by singling out Muslim citizens from everyone else, and that the notion of citizenship is not neutral either: it is constructed through categories of "good" and "bad" that currently exclude Muslims from national belonging, but which historically have also excluded other nonwhite minorities. After each point, instead of responding, he would change the subject and move to another topic. When I responded to that, he would change the topic yet again and move to something else.

In the course of these avoidance tactics, he landed on Quebec, which also happens to be where I did my Ph.D. research on Muslim communities in Montreal. Being unaware that this was an area of expertise for me, he gave an example of how Muslims were using the law in Quebec to have their "demands" met through reasonable accommodation. I challenged this point; reasonable accommodation did not specifically refer to Muslims in the law. It was mobilized as a political and cultural discourse that was used to demarcate the boundaries of belonging between white majorities and racialized, religious minorities.

The discussion moderator tried to interrupt me to make me stop, but I held up my hand and asked him to let me finish the point that I was making and continued. When I finished speaking, the speaker said yes, politics was important. It was a way to appear to agree with me and to end the conversation. I was dismissed.

In this way, he demonstrated intellectually what he had previously embodied physically: the shifting gaze that did not see or engage with me. His intellectual gaze did not acknowledge me as a scholar with expertise on these issues. I was the Muslim subject, he was the white male academic, and his expertise mattered. What I said wasn't of enough import to be engaged with in any substantive fashion.

Academics of color are constantly placed in this space of being hypervisible on one hand, and invisible on the other. We are "native informants" when it is convenient, when it comes to doing research *on* our communities. As one of the few Muslim academics of color in a white university, I run the risk of being seen as a "representative of my people," whichever "people" they may be: sometimes women, sometimes brown women, sometimes Muslims, sometimes Muslim women.

At the same time, when my scholarly work engages critically with these questions of Muslim subjectivity, then it can be conveniently ignored or sidelined because it challenges institutional whiteness and Orientalist privilege. The white male academic is the "expert" and we academics of color are there to receive his "expertise" without too much "talking back" (hooks, 1989). "Good Muslim" subjects (Mamdani, 2004) don't talk back.

When I spoke to him afterward, I introduced myself as part of the research center that was hosting him. He had met my colleagues earlier that day. He told me he had been invited by his colleague from a university in a small town outside of Montreal to visit in three months' time, so he was reading up on the Quebec Charter of Values. It was part of an ongoing political debate focused on Muslims in Quebec. One white colleague in a small town in rural Quebec was inviting this man, another white colleague from Europe to come be an "expert" on the Quebec Charter of Values with him. Through telling me about this invitation, he was in fact underlining to me, the Muslim subject, his position as a white expert on Muslims. I wished him luck with his reading.

This brings me to the system of knowledge production and its circulation in universities, which postcolonial scholar Edward Said critiqued more than 30 years ago. Said pointed out that knowledge about Islam, Muslims, and the Orient is only considered to be knowledge when it is mediated through Western "experts" (Said, 1978, 13). This guest speaker incident exemplifies this dynamic. But, this center is also part of it, and therefore, *you* are also part of it.

This center is in a white university that claims to engage critically with the "Muslim question" in the world today. It includes some Muslim scholars of color whose expertise is in that critique. Yet, our presence, collectively and individually, is contested. Senior staff have told us in staff meetings that there are "too many Muslims" in this center. A senior administrator once told me that I'm not "allowed" to work on my research area.

As a white male administrator, you are complicit in maintaining this structure of white and Orientalist privilege in this university, although this privilege is invisible to you. You make decisions about whose voices and whose work are privileged to speak on "the Muslim question," even though it is not your field. You constantly ask me to explain my research and to justify its existence in the center. At the same time, you host academics like this guest speaker from Europe whose "knowledge" and expertise as a white expert is unquestioned. His research is already considered valuable enough that he is invited and hosted here in the first place.

You, this center, and this university help to maintain a system of knowledge production and circulation that privileges white experts and their "knowledge" about Muslims as part of the hegemonic Orientalist discourse about Muslims. The "knowledge" of these white experts is treated as more legitimate and objective as "knowledge," at the expense of Muslim scholars of color. To add insult to injury, these experts can't even deign to look at us when they speak about us.

I am writing this letter to share what happened at one event because I am unwilling to let my expertise be dismissed and ignored by white male academics in this university. But this incident is part of a much larger structure, which you do not see but you are complicit with. So I am also writing to hold you accountable for your role in maintaining white and Orientalist privilege in this university. As a "good Muslim," I am "talking back."

Sincerely,
Uzma Jamil
A Muslim Scholar of Color

REFERENCES

hooks, b. 1989. *Talking Back: Thinking Feminist, Thinking Black*. Boston: South End Press.
Mamdani, M. 2004. *Good Muslim, Bad Muslim: America, the Cold War, and the Roots of Terror*. New York: Pantheon Books.
Said, E. 1978. *Orientalism*. London: Penguin.

LETTER 21

Hello, Black Women's Lives (Don't) Matter in the Academy.

I am a 45-year-old, black, female, feminist, academic, first-generation college graduate. I speak openly about the third-class status that has been assigned to black women in American society. I am usually silent about the fact that this same third-class status has been assigned to me in academia, but every day I painfully refuse and resist this treatment. The stigmatizing and labeling of black women in academia is an acceptable mode of operating and an unsophisticated old trick of the white-privilege trade. I also acknowledge black men and women's complicity within this white, racist, patriarchal structure.

Black women's academic oppressions are real. The intricate interweaving of racism, sexism, classism, patriarchy, capitalism, and misogyny within and beyond academia aids in black women's disenfranchisement and literal death. I recall the afternoon when one of you said to me, "You know why you are on the grant." I gazed with curiosity and responded, "Why's that?" She said, "We needed to have a black person involved." I walked away with a "f*#k you" grin.

I was furious. I emotionally detached from my colleagues for weeks. I wish I could have screamed in the hallway, "I'm here, don't render me, or my scholarship, invisible!" You tend to look right through me. You see, my dear white colleagues, I think you ignore the fact that we have a history of racial and gendered tension and it is still difficult to trust you. I am expected to excel in my career and work twice as hard to prove my competence. You don't need to do that; you are automatically, intrinsically trusted.

Many of you have managed to forget about the practice, research, and community engagement experience I bring into the academy. Yet, I know all of you by name because of your scholarly work. It sounds like a small matter to you, but it plays into the perceptions that my grandmother and aunt warned me of. "Why must you go into academia," they asked me. "It's no place for us (black women)."

You are not interested in your black, female colleagues. We don't exist: you only see us when you need something or if you are looking to study our people. But perhaps the bigger problem is the lack of acknowledgement of the accomplishments that I, as a black woman, make to the field. Once again I want to scream: "Sometimes I feel that you don't see my accomplishments; they are overshadowed by my skin color, by my jezebel. You are not open to my suggestions or feedback because you don't know me, you don't value my work. You refuse to know me; you persist in formally rejecting me."

I remember sitting in a research meeting where colleagues were asked to provide feedback on a research article drafted by another colleague. The analysis under consideration happened to be in an area where I am well published. I attempted to critique and offer suggestions in the conversation many times. I even explicitly stated, "I've written a few articles that might be great models for your work." My words went unacknowledged, each time. I am left to wonder if this happened because I am a black, proud feminist, one who "kicks ass and takes no names"? Or did this happen because I am invisible, undervalued as an academic colleague?

These subtle, multiplicative microaggressions are draining. I walked away beating myself up, asking myself, "What should have I said? What should have I done?" This quickly passed, giving way to feelings of humiliation, discomfort, isolation, anxiety, and pain. The not so subtle message I got from that experience was, how dare I think of myself as a first-rate scholar? I often, if temporarily, lose the desire to contribute fully to my scholarship, to the academic community. I tell myself, "I am going to continue to be first-rate," because that's apparently the worst offense for black women in the academy.

I suspect that you are not aware of what you're doing. That will remain my assumption until we start to talk openly and honestly about your behavior and treatment of me and people like me. I'm still here, because I want to be here and I'm hoping for institutional shifts.

In the words of Audre Lorde,

> My anger is a response to racist attitudes and to the actions and presumptions that arise out of those attitudes. If your dealings with other women reflect those attitudes, then my anger and your attendant fears are spotlights that can be used for growth in the same way I have used learning to express anger for my growth. (Lorde, 1984, 124)

In the past, I've borne the racist-patriarchal system of academia where I must produce and provide. I've survived. I've reached that moment where it's become draining and physically unbearable; the weight on my shoulders is a burden I am no longer eager to carry. Eight years post-tenure, I am still practicing survival mechanisms—from pouring out my struggles to (un)trustworthy colleagues, closing the office door and crying by myself to myself, unapologetically forcing my racist-patriarchal frustrations in departmental conversations, to flooding the ears of allies and friends. This is tiring. As my sister-friend Beverly Guy-Sheftall reminds me, "Give yourself permission to be angry." I'm angry, but I am tired of being angry.

In my office, you will find pictures of beautiful, radical-feminist-queer-unapologetic, black women: to name a few, Beverly Guy-Sheftall, Angela Davis, Cheryl Clarke, Paula Giddings, Alice Walker, Pearl Cleage, Dorcey Applyrs, and of course, me. I intentionally make my space breathe "black women's lives matter." Make no mistake—a black woman works, lives, and breathes here. These things have nothing to do with my research and everything to do with my personal, spiritual, and political survival at this institution. I am affirmed by my space, in your space. This works for me.

Unapologetically,
Lani V. Jones, Ph.D., L.C.S.W.

REFERENCES

Guy-Sheftall, B. 2014. "The First Person—Being a 'Good Girl' and the Importance of Talking Back." Women*etics*, May.
Lorde, Audre. 1984. "The Uses of Anger: Women Responding to Racism." In *Sister Outsider: Essays and Speeches*. New York: Crossing Press.

LETTER 22

Dear Junior Scholar,

Welcome to the academy, or "the club," as a well-wisher whispered into my ear upon the successful defense of my dissertation! As a new club member, you have joined a collective of smart people responsible for crafting and promoting ideas, informing policy, and shaping minds. This club, called "higher education," is a distinct entity entrenched in neoclassical curricula and modern-day bureaucracy. If you are a woman like me—confident, progressive, black, unconventional—most assuredly you will encounter review, resistance, but eventual reward. Fortunately, my unrelenting exercise of the aforementioned characteristics buoyed me to tenure amid an unwelcoming climate. Having worked through that resistance, I offer you a bit of advice and affirmation.

First, pursue scholarship that interests you! What interests you will engage you, and personal interest is self-sustaining. Presumably you have spent the last five to ten years "married" to a research question. Such dedication is essential, because the answer to your question is intended to launch your scholarship. Unfortunately, this launch-to-scholarship connection was *not* whispered into my ear.

At the onset of my tenure-track gig, I attempted to utilize my qualitative dissertation data. However, since I wasn't deeply "feeling" the project as a doctoral candidate, that disinterest accompanied me to the academy. Despite identifying a fresh theoretical frame or applying a different analytical lens, my efforts to write accepted peer-review journal manuscripts fell flat.

My concern for the lived experiences of the eight white teacher candidates "Learning to Teach among Schoolchildren of Color" (Davis, 2004) had evaporated. I was detached from the research and removed from its familiar New England milieu. The scholastic "big town" perspectives that cultivated my liberal, deep-seated, African American identity affirming the dissertation project had been supplanted by an uber-global marketplace serviced by a lot of "us." Despite low percentages of brown and black folk in *my* club, high percentages of "us" *served* club members. Frequently people expected me in facilities rather than *on* faculty. Sometimes I wasn't even expected, particularly during field supervision.

My teaching load included supervising elementary school student teachers. As a transplant, most of the schools were in unfamiliar communities. Once, after getting lost, I faced difficulty situating myself within an elementary school. As I approached the building's side door, I saw a white male custodian on the inside. I smiled, waved, then pulled the door handle; but the door was locked. Rather than open the door, the custodian wagged his finger at me, then used it to motion me around the building. Afterward he turned, walked away from the door, and out of my view.

Inside the building, I passed a white woman who greeted me. Walking in the opposite direction, she used her finger to motion me toward the office. There, I introduced myself to the white office secretary who said, "I'm surprised you didn't see the principal in the hallway—she just left." Moments later the principal called the secretary asking who I was and what I wanted. Apparently the woman pointing me toward the office was the school principal—but what had prevented her from questioning me in the hallway? What of me frightened her?

Subsequent unwelcoming school encounters led me to direct my students, "Please tell the white administrators in your clinical sites that your black professor is coming to observe you!" Given some students' sensitivity, I figured the admonition would have implications likely to label me a racist, but I deemed the caution necessary. Recurring chilly receptions led me to inform my department chair that I would no longer supervise candidates in predominantly white communities.

At the time, I considered those frigid receptions from school personnel isolated slights. Surely on campus my club membership would be obvious and respected. In reality, those school incidents represented both subtle, unintentional snubs of microaggressions and blatant, purposeful rebuffs of macroaggressions without boundaries. In fact, on campus, the insults continued and intensified.

One evening I was en route to my car parked in a lot reserved for full-time employees. Planning to take an evening yoga class, I was wearing sneakers and yoga pants. A white male faculty member saw me and bellowed, "You don't belong in this lot, it's for faculty and staff; you're not allowed to park in here. I oughta have you towed!" Stunned, I initially kept quiet for fear of saying something to further upset the "wrong person." He could have been a senior administrator cunning enough to use his white male privilege to retaliate against me.

Mindful of that possibility, I calmly responded, "I'm okay to park here." Perhaps having a bad day, expecting an angry or complaint black woman his aggression intensified, leading him to summon a parking attendant. Then, in another instance of finger pointing, the faculty member asserted, "I want that black son-of-a-bitch ticketed and towed." Now *he* had upset the wrong sister! Weeks later, upon my recommendation, human resources officers directed the aggressor to write a letter of apology still displayed on my office wall. His letter functions as a cautionary tale against cultural insensitivity on my campus.

Along with chilly receptions and finger wagging, pejorative euphemisms prevail in the academy. The persistent use of "minority" rubs me so much that I wrote a poem about it. The abstract reads,

> Among scholars, practitioners, politicians, and the media, the term "minority" is often used to refer to people of color—human beings of African . . . descent. However . . . minority means the smaller part or number . . . less than half. Minority suggests diminution. [True, certain] groups are *in* the minority because they are not part of the racial, ethnic and political majority in the United States . . . . But is it appropriate to use a group's statistical representation . . . as a euphemism for their identity? Besides, [who] are [the] . . . "majorities"? (Davis, 2009, 491)

"Inner-city" and "urban" are equally loaded terms. Over time, these terms have become euphemisms for brown and black people. Despite the zip code or setting, "inner-city" and "urban" often function as encryption, chiefly for youth of color living and learning in underserved communities. This negative messaging disturbs me because I grew up in the city—see Davis, 2008. Yet, many students in my classes discredit my academic achievements and disagree with my pedagogy.

Some discount my wide-ranging childhood experiences, such as the time an older, white, female student naïvely asked, "Had you seen a tree-lined street before you came to our community?" Although personally irksome, these incidents need public disclosure—especially for peers and scholars espousing principles of social justice, equity, and democracy. There is still work to do.

Writing about micro- and macroaggressions has become part of my scholarship. The scholarship borrows from two qualitative research tools, autoethnography and critical race theory (CRT), which segue to my second piece of advice. Your scholarship can uniquely narrate *your* story. I dub these writings autoethnographic narrative poetry (ANP). Unlike form poetry, ANP consists of multiple pages, unique forms, and rhythms organized to authenticate my lived experience. Speaking about my scholarship, a good colleague—a turn of phrase I coined to signal a close friend in the academy—advised, "You're not gonna get tenure writing poems." Perhaps that mentality brands her a rock-star researcher and marks me a soldier scholar. Nonetheless, I maintain my commitment to my form of choice.

Like many female scholars of African descent, my scholarship is relative to my cultural background and personal experiences (Ladson-Billings and Donnor, 2005; Stanley, 2007). As a black female scholar, I recognize that all voices and perspectives are not respected in traditional scholarship, justifying alternative approaches. During my tenure review, I experienced yet another slight when the dean of my college "minoritized" my scholarship by diminishing my work. While celebrating and embracing my diversity—especially for affirmative action purposes and website marketing—she rendered my nontraditional scholarship insignificant, ultimately reducing me to invisibility.

With its erudite referents of higher education, the academy, and the ivory tower, for sisters like me, *club* membership is dolefully challenging yet distinctively fulfilling. Expect colleagues, students, and the community to question you—*out of* ignorance and *because* they are ignorant. The academy's distinctiveness requires knowing *yourself* and identifying *your* needs for success. To that end, consider the business practice of strategic positioning.

Strategic positioning involves deciding where you'd like to be in six to seven years, the common tenure timeline. Next, inventory your current situation, identify present, and future opportunities; then figure out how those opportunities will advance you. For implementation, determine whether you are a conventional scholar, a trailblazer, or somewhere in the middle. To navigate the challenges that will come, find a good colleague for solace and support. Remember that the academy prides itself on neoclassical practices, so your decision to work around those expectancies will certainly result in opposition—trust me, I know!

Whether you align yourself with unconventionality or tradition, select a space respectful of your lived experience *and* your scholarship—or amenable to honestly respecting your life and your work.

Sincerely,
Professor Davis

REFERENCES

Davis, D. 2009. "Being in the Minority Is My Circumstance Not My Identity." *African Identities* 7(4): 491–94.

Davis, D. 2008. The Inner City Is My Blues. *Multicultural Education* 15(2): 28–29.

Davis, D. 2004. "Learning to Teach among Schoolchildren of Color" (Doctoral dissertation, Boston College). *Dissertation Abstracts International* 65, 3. (UMI 3126373).

Ladson-Billings, G. J. and Donnor, J. K. 2005. "Waiting for the Call: The Moral Activist Role of Critical Race Theory Scholarship." In Denzin, N. K. and Lincoln, Y. S. (eds.), *Handbook of Qualitative Research.* 3rd ed., 279–301). Thousand Oaks, CA: Sage.

LETTER 23

Dear Fellow Members of the Academy and Higher Education, (or, A Letter from the Ivory Tower)

When I entered graduate school at Cornell University, I thought I knew a thing or two about racism. After all, I am a colored girl raised in the South with the Civil Rights Movement at my back. The assassination of Martin Luther King and school desegregation stoked my emergent political consciousness. But for more than three decades, the academy would teach me a great deal about American racism—it was to be a deeply painful education.

Racism all but crushed my spirit, and it nearly threatened my life. I grew fat, tired, and sick in the defense of my name and that which was most deeply personal to me—my intellect, character, and voice. Racism attacked all that made me most whole as a scholar and as a person. I was raised to work harder, be better, to excel, and to achieve—but this neither saved nor protected me.

I believe in redemption and forgiveness, just as much as I once believed in the power of excellence as an antidote to narratives of black inferiority that crept so effortlessly into the consciousness of those around me. So, when I could take no more, I wondered, often aloud, what of their God?

Racism is a sifter that sustains racial inequity—a churning morass of ways of thinking, rituals, practices, beliefs, language, and ethical solipsism that is at once vaguely present and totalizing. And racism, like many ordinary things, passes easily for nothingness.

Still, racism contorts and disfigures; the scars, if not apparent on our bodies, are borne by our souls. Yet, racism is not personal. This is a paradoxical truth, I know. What the academy taught me is that racism is no respecter of persons. This is true for those who must endure its wrath and for those who are its instruments.

Racism, whatever its innovations, hides within the normalcy of sameness. This is reminiscent of Bill Murray's *Groundhog Day* (1993), except that the protagonist fails to learn its lessons, and the town never changes. Things go on, repeating themselves ad infinitum. Whatever disruptions that may have occurred today are forgotten tomorrow, with no cumulative effect.

There was a time when I began to believe that racism was magical; as no one else could remember we had been right at this place before, saying all the same words, for the same reasons. We were entranced or bewitched; I was never sure which.

What the academy taught me was that racism needs repetition; repetition is its lifeblood. Repetition normalizes racism's practices and its inequities, and it is through repetition that racism derives its moral authority and soothes all ambivalences, leaving nothing to be forgiven.

Not too long ago, I found a letter I wrote as a graduate student to my department's faculty. The onion-skin paper was littered with fuzzy serifs from my old typewriter. Within it, I made my first cogent arguments to support faculty diversity—all have grown old to me now—beneath which was the almost prayer to see us/me as valued humans and as scholars capable of rich intellectual thought.

In the 11,332 mornings since I placed that letter into faculty mailboxes, everything and nothing has changed, and the thought of this grieves me.

I have seen colleagues, mostly liberals, wrestle with the yoke of racism. I have felt the earnestness of their struggle and too often witnessed its futility. What I learned is that racism in the most destructive way completes us.

I appealed to the liberal sensibilities and values within the academy, but liberalism is unlikely to disrupt racism, and it is often an enabler. This is made no more evident than by the near-ubiquitous trope of the Qualified Minority, who is apparently as elusive as Big Foot and as dangerous as the Boogie Man.

Critical race theorists—notably Derrick Bell, Kimberlé Crenshaw, Patricia Williams, and Mari Matsuda—argue that racially codified meritocracy and white-sensitive colorblindness not only impede liberal efforts but also leave intact ideological and institutional practices through which racial inequities persist. What the academy taught me is just how seductive racism can be, and this I never imagined.

A seduction that is more primal than ideology, more sensual than political—an allure often more powerful than any resistance or all of our professed values that stand in opposition.

I have seen racism coddled, protected, and even loved—and this is a dangerous thing to say. But, I witnessed the satiation that comes when racism has its fill, and no measure of shame or guilt stops us from returning there.

As a child, I remember watching the documentary *King: A Filmed Record, Montgomery to Memphis*; and though uplifted by the black struggle, it was Bull Connor I studied. I thought him to be an immoral man. I now understand the ugliness of Connor's resistance was in measure to the immorality of what he sought to protect, which he loved more than heaven itself.

Racism is an unruly lover that both draws and repels. The academy taught me that racism is hard to give up, no matter the collective cost; and this is no less true of well-educated liberals than it was of Bull Connor.

Nearly two decades ago, Jim Sleeper's *Liberal Racism* critiqued liberal intellectuals for expecting too little and too much of "nonwhites" like me; but liberal politics did not lead to new forms of racism, nor could the acknowledgement of racial-ethnic identities absolve the old.

Marginal shifts in curriculum, faculty rosters, and student bodies left intact the everyday and systemic practices that sustain racial inequities within institutions of higher learning. These transformations are less than imagined, and perhaps hoped for, but comforted, we fell mostly silent about race—as if racism was a scab that would heal leaving no scars if we stopped picking it.

It recently occurred to me that I would no more use the R-word than the N-word in polite academic company. I do not know when this happened, but racism has become *That-Which-Should-Not-Be-Named*. This absence of naming leaves racism disembodied, less real, and unattached to human actors—leaving no place to start or finish its undoing.

I am reminded of *G. G. McLaurin and Some of His Kin*, a text I read for my genealogical research. The author writes that his grandmother, a God-fearing woman who likely owned my kin, said, "If the slaves wanted to leave or run away there was nothing to stop them," reducing slavery to the personal choice of those in bondage, with no mention of all that held what was in place.

What I learned is that racial inequity is also managed in higher education as if there is no agency; thus, we are not accountable for what is. Then and now, racism *is* because we have made it so—but we loathe to own what we have created.

And the most hopeful and painful lesson the academy taught me is that in matters of race, there is only what we have done, will do, or not—and that is a mindful practice.

Mindfully Yours in Peace, Hope, and Equity,
Andrea G. Hunter, Ph.D.

REFERENCE

McLaurin, G. G. 1970. *G. G. McLaurin and Some of His Kin: Sketches and Genealogy.* Washington, DC.

Chapter Fifteen

Mentor Essay

The Talk

Eduardo Bonilla-Silva, Duke University

Our enemies are not that big, what happens is that we are kneeling. Let's stand
up.
—Ramón Emeterio Betances, 19th-century Puerto Rican separatist leader

I wish someone had given me "the talk" when I landed in Madison, Wisconsin, in 1984 to pursue a Ph.D. in sociology. Although Professor Charles
Camic was a truly wonderful adviser, neither he nor any of the few sociologists of color in Madison at the time sat me down to tell me how race would
affect my academic voyage. Accordingly, I navigated my first few years in
graduate school like a blind man.

Racially motivated things happened and I could not read them correctly.
What were all these things about? Were Americans rude to me because I was
an AmeRícan? ("AmeRícan" is a poem by black Puerto Rican poet Tato
Laviera. See his *AmeRícan.* Houston: Arte Público Press, 1985.) Were all
these things due to "cultural differences"? As a Puerto Rican, I am an
American citizen, but I was born in Bellefonte, Pennsylvania, in 1962. However, Puerto Ricans from the island (and I grew up there) have a totally
different culture from Americans; hence, I attributed a lot of things to cultural differences.

I saw Chicano students and African Americans languish in the program.
Our survival rate was significantly lower than that of our white peers, but our
early exits were always labeled as sui generis cases ("Precious left because
she was not truly a sociologist" or "Marta did not have what it takes"). No
one dared to say there was a "structural race factor" behind our high academic mortality. But, somehow, I did not perish. I self-trained in race through my

involvement in racial struggles at the university in the late 1980s and reading intensively for a race course I taught in the early 1990s. I connected the dots and understood that race matters everywhere we transact life. Thus, by the late 1980s, I was ready for racial prime time.

Now, some thirty years after my initial disorienting entrance into the Amerikan Akademy,[1] I have the expertise to give "the talk" to my students. First, I underscore the fact that they are in an HWCU (Historically Black College and/or University) and that, as such, the organizational and political structure of the institution is fundamentally shaped by whiteness. Sociology departments, no matter how much they see themselves as "progressive," reproduce organizational whiteness in their curriculum, hiring practices, norms, events, and even in the food they order for parties.

Second, I disabuse them of the idea that fellow, white, graduate students and faculty will treat them as their equals. In many direct and indirect ways, they will feel this differential treatment. Most tell me later that they have indeed had what Elijah Anderson (2011) has termed as "the nigger moment": the moment when a white student or professor said or did something that made clear to them that the white student or professor regard us as "inferior," as one-sided scholars only interested in race. This realization is always harder when the discriminator is one of their professors. Faculty are supposed to be neutral and treat their students equally. But how do you process the facts of your life: such as when your statistics professor refuses to help you and you learn later that he has been helping some of your fellow white students?

Third, I explain to them that because whites form a quasi-kin group, they will not invite them to activities, events, study groups, and the like. Although they will not be excluded from formal things in the department, they will experience informal exclusion—a form of exclusion that has tremendous consequences for their sociological life chances. Hence, I advise them to bond with fellow students of color in the department and elsewhere, as black and brown survival is key. It usually takes students a month of being in the program to understand that the love they felt during the recruitment period is gone! I also tell them that no matter how alienated they feel, they must show up to events, and parties and do their best to interact with white faculty and white students. Why? Because sociology is white dominated and we cannot just proceed ignoring this fundamental social fact.

Fourth, I encourage my students to work with any white professor willing to work with them. Many of my students do not understand or appreciate this advice early, but later on, they get it. They realize that because whites rule the academy, they will need networks and support from them to do well in this business. It is virtually impossible to graduate from a sociology department without having some form of white backing.

For example, if a student of color just has letters of recommendation from faculty of color, whites discount these letters as biased; their assumption is that we support students of color out of racial solidarity. Of course, white students routinely have exclusively white faculty writing letters for them and no one ever says, "These letters come only from white folks, so they reflect just a racial solidarity thing."

Fifth, I tell them that although I have some networks and standing in the discipline, they must also understand that there is a (mostly) white sociological elite that rules the discipline. This white elite dominates top departments, top journals, funding agencies, academic presses, and most sociology organizations—particularly, the American Sociological Association. (Even when people like me get elected president of this association, the organizational power, rules of engagement, and cultural practices remain the same, so our election changes little, and in a curious way, ends up legitimizing the organization.) I tell them all this because I want them to develop practices that will give them options.

For instance, if they wish to get an NSF grant or a Ford fellowship, I urge them to vet their applications with white faculty. Why? Because white faculty have the racialized sociological capital (white faculty do not know their "sociological capital" is a racialized asset) that will help my students figure things out and write in such a way that the likely white readers of their applications will find compelling.

Sixth, I do my best to explain to my students the emotional consequences of laboring in these places. It is very hard to work in organizations where one is not viewed or treated as an equal. Although as race scholars we know (or should know) this fact, experiencing treatment as "second class sociologists" kills us a little every day. I tell them that although I am now viewed by many as an accomplished scholar, I suffer the same trauma they do.

I too feel exclusion; I hear through the rumor mill painful things, such as a former ASA president who said that I am not good because I am "political," or a colleague who classified the work I do as "me-search" rather than research. Because I know *en carne propia* that these things hurt, I have an open-door policy on these matters. My students may come to my office or call me to talk about their racial pain. I work to let them know that we will get through whatever they are going through together!

Seventh, I let my students know that I am there for them 100 percent. They know I will do the best I can to make sure they finish their Ph.D. Letting students know they can count on me for everything is crucial as most students of color come from poor or working-class backgrounds and deal with the class-race consequences of their location. They deal with financial issues such as not being able to pay a medical fee because their deductible still is too high or having family members asking them to help them with bills. And although some white students come from poor and working-class backgrounds (I am there for them, too), my students of color must deal with racism on top of their class-based injuries.

This is the basic talk I give to my students and am proud that I have graduated ten students so far (nine of them students of color) and have seven who will graduate soon. Although at some level I wish I did not have to give this talk to them (wouldn't it be great if we were truly color-blind and could just focus on sociology stuff?), I am pragmatic enough to know that without this lifesaver, many would literally drown. The talk is necessary because race matters intensely in the akademy.

REFERENCES

Anderson, E. 2011. *The Cosmopolitan Canopy: Race and Civility in Everyday Life*. New York: W. W. Norton.
Laviera. T 1985. *AmeRícan*. Houston: Arte Público Press.

NOTE

1. I choose to spell Amerika with a "k," a choice that offends some. But, as I explain in my book, *Racism without Racists*, I stylize it this way in order to signify that race is central to the construction of this nation: where the racism was perhaps explicit in "AmeriKKKa," I suggest, Amerika cannot escape the legacy of its racist/racialized path. Some (including those in the academy) may play the silly game that we somehow are above the social fray. This is impossible, and thus my notion of both the country and the Amerikan Akademy as race-central institutions are represented in this spelling.

Afterword

The Historical Moment

As we complete this volume in the summer of 2016, social media news feeds are flooded with the stories of two black fathers who were murdered in cold blood at the hands of police officers. Alton Sterling and Philando Castile are the latest additions to the long list of innocent black and brown men and women who have been murdered by police. From the inception of this project in the fall of 2014, dozens of lives have been lost from police and private citizen violence.

As we received letters from faculty across the country, we were also opening Internet tabs to read the stories of the nine African American church members killed by a white supremacist in South Carolina; the Orlando night club shooting that took the lives of 49 mostly queer patrons, many of who were black and Latino; and the rise of a presidential candidate's anti-Mexican, Islamophobic political platform. Simultaneously, the Black Lives Matter movement has emerged as a neo–Civil Rights movement—only to be met by "all lives matter" counter-narratives.

Why are we talking about these events in a small volume, which may or may not be widely read by the general public, on the experiences of faculty of color in higher education? Similar to the Civil Rights Movement, the Black Lives Matter movement has found its legs with young people on college campuses across the country and abroad. This volume's original goal was to paint a vivid portrait of the assaults that faculty of color negotiate and their subsequent triumphs, despite considerable obstacles in places where the outside world might least expect them: in the battlefield of the classroom. And while the university system and college campuses are relatively protected spaces compared to city and suburban streets, and as faculty, faculty of color occupy a (semi) privileged position, the classroom is nonetheless a contested space.

Bonilla–Silva's mentor letter, titled "The Talk" reminds us that America was built on white domination, and all institutions and interactions flow from this structural reality. In a university system that was built on slavery-based capitalism, it is not surprising that faculty of color have a "third-class citizenship" in the hierarchy of the ivory tower. What is surprising, and is reflected in the content of many of the letters in this volume, are the countless public and private interactions that render faculty of color voiceless, disempowered, and marginalized although they are told that they have joined "the club."

In what Howard Winant describes as the "break" in racial domination, white supremacy has found ways to reinvent itself in the face of mass movements for racial justice. One of the strategies in the "dualism of white supremacy" is the inclusion of small numbers of nonwhites in exclusively white professions. The contradiction in "minority representation" is that the systems of white control over decision-making, resources, and prestige remain largely intact.

This is also true in academia. While many faculty of color have been able to ascend the ranks, contributors to *Stories* remind us that many more scholars of color never make it to full professor, or simply exit the academy all together. Therefore, what this volume has demonstrated to all of its editors is that, despite the pervasiveness of the particularities that hinder faculty of color's advancement and social well-being, a fundamental problem is racism.

The United States struggles to reconcile the increasing minority population within its neighborhoods, workplaces, and churches with its historical racial ghosts. And while police stops and the mysterious deaths of men and women of color while in police custody are indicative of the abuses of white controlled police forces against black and brown communities, professors and their families are in no way exempt from racial profiling and what Anderson (2011) calls the "nigger moment." These moments, when all pretense of civility is lost, can be experienced by any individual with provisional status.

Ersula Ore, a black female professor at Arizona State University, was slammed to the ground for jaywalking on campus when she was trying to avoid walking near a construction site. Imani Perry, a black Princeton professor, was taken into custody for a traffic ticket she never received. Henry Louis Gates, perhaps the first faculty member to bring national attention to these injustices for faculty, was arrested in front of his home near Harvard's campus in 2009. For speaking truth to power on Twitter, Saida Grundy was harassed by conservative white students who didn't think her opinions on the toxicity of white male culture on college campuses were appropriate for a college professor.

The narratives in this volume provide countless other events in which the deficit of credibility that faculty of color encounter is named. From students who are not comfortable with the Mexicanness of their mathematics professor; to colleagues who informally police public space on campus; to other faculty of color who perpetuate the toxic culture of racial, gendered, and class subjugation in their own right; it will take not another social movement, but a complete reorganization of racial power, to have a racially equal university environment. Until then, the Black and Brown Lives Matter Movement will resonate on the streets of Southside Chicago and University of Missouri all the same. In fact, some might argue that *Stories from the Front of the Room* is itself merely a reflection of this racial dynamic.

However, a careful reading of the letters in this volume shows that it is not just about race, gender, or one position or identity. What these letters illustrate is what many scholarly attempts have failed to do. They unpack all of the statuses, roles, and positions that operate simultaneously that yield the problematic outcomes that faculty of color experience. A Muslim, young, female, upper-middle-class, heterosexual professor is interpreted and treated differently than an Asian, gay, working-class, middle-aged Christian. They occupy different spaces in the social hierarchy of the academy, and sometimes one has more power than the other depending on the context.

In a 2009 TED talk, novelist Chimamanda Adichie warns of the danger of a single story. We, therefore, encourage our readers to think differently about narratives such as those collected here. Reducing the narratives in this volume into a single story—that of racial subjugation or racial triumph— risks cheapening the gifts these authors have so generously given. The narratives are richly layered and textured. From simple stories, we find complex layers of intersectionality.

The 23 contributors whose letters we feature are entering in or have left the academy; are pre- and post-tenure; teach at historically black or traditionally white institutions that are public or private, large, medium, and small; are scholars in the humanities and the behavioral, social, and natural sciences; and most importantly, have spent time in the front of college and university classrooms. In other words, they represent and share characteristics with the faculty of color throughout the United States.

Our call for contributions was distributed through many academic networks including academic conferences and listservs, and of course, through word of mouth. We received more than 50 inquiries/statements of interest, and while we invited almost all of those individuals to submit a letter, a number of colleagues chose not to do so because of time constraints or, in the case of two potential letter writers, because they were ultimately afraid of reprisals if their names were to appear in a letter. An assurance of anonymity was not sufficient inducement; one colleague actually wrote and submitted a letter and then later withdrew it because of fear that the specific setting and the events that were described could identify the letter writer as the lone person of color in a unique space.

Our contributors are courageous men and women who relay experiences that are sometimes cringeworthy and raw. Some reveal the ridiculous exploitation that faculty of color experience not only (or necessarily) as a result of the kinds of labor they are called on to perform in the academy, but also in terms of what their presence brings to the academy—bodies that fill "diversity" quotas. Other letters speak to the paradox of invisibility even as one experiences hypervisibility. All of these letters, from faculty and mentors alike, speak to the incredible resilience, grace, and strength of individuals who labor under less-than-ideal conditions because of their strong belief in the importance of what they do in higher education. We are grateful for their contributions.

In conclusion, it is important to acknowledge that universities are among the most conservative institutions in our society, where change is slow and never guaranteed. It is for this reason that resolving the issues that faculty of color face within the academy will require struggle. Faculty of color will be the ones in the vanguard of this struggle, along with their allies. But just as crucial to this struggle is the need to name the textures and articulations of the injustices faced by faculty of color plainly and provocatively.

REFERENCES

Adichie, Chimamanda Ngozi. 2009. "The Danger of a Single Story." TED Talks. https://www.ted.com/talks/chimamanda_adichie_the_danger_of_a_single_story?language=en. Accessed October 7, 2009.

Anderson, E. 2011. *The Cosmopolitan Canopy: Race and Civility in Everyday Life*. New York: W. W. Norton.

Index

academic freedom, 2
affirmative action, 8, 13–14, 19, 44, 85, 88, 141
active learning, 34, 70
African American, 26, 27, 29–30, 35, 38, 39, 40, 56, 83, 84, 86, 88, 121, 124, 139, 160, 161, 163, 164, 166, 167

class and classism, 1, 4, 5, 16, 18, 19, 29–34, 38, 43–46, 49–52, 55–56, 58–60, 63–64, 66, 70, 72, 80, 85, 86–88, 91–93, 97, 100–107, 123, 129–131, 136, 140, 149, 152, 153, 158, 163, 166
community service, 33
conflict, 4, 6, 53, 82, 130
critical race theory, 141, 157, 165
cultural taxation, 1, 13, 31–32, 77, 99, 129
curriculum, 3, 22, 56, 59, 123, 144, 148, 160, 162

discrimination, 1, 3, 71, 81, 109, 112, 157
diversity, 15, 20, 32, 43, 59, 71–73, 78–81, 97–101, 103–104, 118, 119, 141, 143, 154, 157, 159, 163, 166, 167

early career, 104
equity, 45, 84, 141
ethnicity, 1, 55, 58, 158, 167
evaluations, 44, 46, 47, 52, 60, 65, 69, 70, 86, 91, 99, 106–108, 113–116, 121, 166

faculty research, 70
funding, 15, 52, 99, 120, 149

gender, 1, 5, 15, 16, 19, 27, 43–45, 47, 58, 63–64, 66, 72, 77, 79, 80, 85, 90, 93, 107, 111, 113, 115, 121, 130, 131, 136, 153, 163, 165. *See also* sexism

higher education, 1, 7, 8, 17, 24, 25, 31, 43, 47, 58, 71, 79, 83, 97, 99, 100, 103, 118, 119, 138, 141, 144, 151, 160, 166, 167
Historically Black Colleges and Universities (HBCU), 43, 148
historically white institutions, 3, 131
homophobia, 66

identity, 19, 45, 71, 76, 79, 87, 99, 129, 131, 139, 140, 142, 153, 157, 164, 167
implicit bias, 65
imposter syndrome, 69, 115
intersectionality, 13, 58, 161
Islam and Islamophobia, 135, 151, 163

leadership, 63, 84, 85, 99, 100, 160

marginalization, 13, 54
mentor, 1, 9, 13, 20, 26, 31, 33, 43, 45, 60, 72, 79, 99, 100, 109
microaggressions, 8, 17, 26, 58, 88, 93, 109, 110, 137, 140

promotion, 8, 43, 45, 60, 70–73, 83–85, 97, 114

race, 1, 8, 15–16, 30, 31, 39–40, 44–47, 49, 54, 58, 71, 73, 81, 86, 90, 107, 121, 130–131, 141, 143, 144, 147–149, 153, 158–157, 161–163, 165–167
racism, 2, 3, 8, 15, 19, 26, 27, 29, 46, 52–54, 58–60, 64, 66, 72, 81, 83, 85, 88, 105, 109, 111, 113, 115, 119, 121, 125, 131, 138, 142–144, 159, 160, 165
research, 3, 5, 9, 10, 13–16, 17, 22–25, 33, 37, 43–44, 47, 54–56, 70–73, 76, 86–87, 90–93, 99, 104–105, 114–115, 121, 123, 129–132, 134–139, 144, 149, 157, 159–167

service, 3, 9, 13–15, 33, 38, 40, 43, 69–71, 77–79, 82, 86, 132, 163
sexism, 1, 5, 15, 16, 19, 27, 43–45, 47, 58, 63–64, 66, 72, 77, 79, 80, 85, 90, 93, 107, 111, 113, 115, 121, 130, 131, 136, 153, 163, 165. *See also* gender
social justice, 45, 78, 84, 141, 163, 166
stress, 4, 71, 77, 79, 97, 129, 157

teaching evaluations, 69, 91, 113, 115, 166
tenure, 3, 6–10, 16, 20, 23, 24, 28, 29, 43, 45, 60, 69–73, 75–77, 79, 83–88, 89–90, 90, 92, 93, 97, 103, 114, 120–123, 131, 137–139, 141, 153
token and tokenism, 129
transgender, 64
trauma, 8, 72, 81, 125, 149

About the Editors

MICHELLE HARRIS

Michelle Harris is a Professor in the Department of Africana Studies/Social Welfare at University at Albany. Her scholarly writings have focused on several areas including acculturation and stress among immigrant Americans, how racial discrimination affects the mental health and well-being of blacks in the United States, and the effects of sociodemographic factors and stress on the mental health of Jamaican adults. She has also published in the area of critical race theory. Dr. Harris envisioned and convened the first Working Group on Emergent Identities (2010) when her research interest shifted to issues of identity construction and performance among indigenous peoples around the world. *The Politics of Identity: Emerging Indigeneity* (2013) was coedited by Dr. Harris and is one scholarly product, among several, of the Working Group.

SHERRILL L. SELLERS

Sherrill L. Sellers is a Professor and Associate Dean in the College of Education, Health & Society at Miami University in Oxford, Ohio. She studies the mental and physical health consequences of social inequalities; intersections of race, genetics, and health; and aging and the life course. She specializes in mixed methods, scale development, and the formation and assessment of diversity and inclusion teaching and training efforts. Her published works appear in *American Journal of Public Health, Journal of Health and Social Behavior*, and *Genetics and Medicine*, among others. Sellers frequently reviews articles for leading journals and has sat on multiple editorial boards, such as *Issues in Race and Society: An International, Global Journal*. Most recently, she coedited a volume, *Research Methodologies in Black Communities*.

ORLY CLERGE

Orly Clerge is an Assistant Professor in the Department of Sociology and Africana Studies at Tufts University in Medford, Massachusetts. She studies how minority populations negotiate their position in the American social hierarchy, with a particular emphasis on how middle-class black families manage their racial, class, and ethnic identities in everyday life. Orly is broadly interested in the areas of race and ethnicity, immigration and migration, urban sociology and social demography. Dr. Clerge's work has appeared in *Ethnic and Racial Studies* and *Sociology Compass.*

FREDERICK W. GOODING JR.

Frederick W. Gooding Jr. is an Assistant Professor within the Ethnic Studies Program at Northern Arizona University in Flagstaff, Arizona. A trained historian, Gooding most effectively analyzes contemporary mainstream media with a careful eye for persistent patterns along racial lines that appear benign but indeed have problematic historical roots. Uncomfortable with the anti-intellectualist approach to hip-hop within academia, Gooding has also fostered new learning opportunities for students and community members to appreciate the genius of hip-hop through new courses, seminars, and study tours abroad. A developing scholar, Gooding's most well-known work thus far is *You Mean, There's RACE in My Movie? The Complete Guide to Understanding Race in Mainstream Hollywood* that critically analyzes the value and impact of contemporary racial imagery based upon historical narratives of sex, power and violence.

About the Contributors

AMANISHAKETE ANI

Dr. Amani Ani is an intellectual warrior for Pan African health and consciousness in society. Her current research program involves strengthening the Black family via the protection of Black women's wombs as the community's key source of both spiritual and creative vitality. She teaches in the areas of racism, ethos, quantitative research methods, and Black community development, with specific focus on Africana families. To date, Dr. Ani has published articles in the *Journal of Black Studies*, *Journal of Black Psychology*, *Journal of Negro Education*, and the *Journal of Pan African Studies*, as well as a book with African American Images.

JUAN BATTLE

Juan Battle is a Professor of Sociology, Public Health, & Urban Education at the Graduate Center of the City University of New York (CUNY). He is also the Coordinator of the Africana Studies Certificate Program. His research focuses on race, sexuality, and social justice (see www.juanbattle.com).

CARLOTTA A. BERRY

Carlotta A. Berry is an Associate Professor in the Department of Electrical and Computer Engineering at Rose-Hulman Institute of Technology. She is the Director of the Multidisciplinary Minor in Robotics and Co-Director of the NSF S-STEM Rose Building Undergraduate Diversity (ROSE-BUD) Program. She has a bachelor's degree in mathematics and electrical engineering from Spelman College and Georgia Institute of Technology. She has a master's degree in electrical engineering from Wayne State University and a Ph.D. in electrical engineering from Vanderbilt University. Her research interests are in robotics education, interface design, human-robot interaction, and increasing underrepresented populations in STEM fields. Dr. Berry has taught undergraduate courses in Human-Robot Interaction, Mobile Robotics, circuits, controls, and freshman and senior design. She has been the president of the Technical Editor Board for the ASEE (American Society for Engineering Education) *Computers in Education Journal*, secretary and treasurer in IEEE (Institute of Electrical and Electronics Engineers) Central Indiana Section, IEEE Central Tennessee Section, and ASEE Mind Division. She is a member of ASEE, IEEE, NSBE, and Eta Kappa Nu.

EDUARDO BONILLA-SILVA

Eduardo Bonilla-Silva is Chair and Professor of Sociology at Duke University. His 1996 article in the *American Sociological Review*, "Rethinking Racism: Toward a Structural Interpretation," where he advanced a materialist interpretation of racial affairs, helped change the way social analysts frame and interpret racial outcomes. He is the author of *Racism without Racists*, *White Logic, White Methods*, and *White Supremacy and Racism in the Post-Civil Rights Era*, among others. He has received several awards from organizations such as the American Sociological Association, most notably, the 2011 Cox-Johnson-Frazier Award for work in the tradition of these black scholars.

TAMIKA CAREY

Tamika L. Carey, Ph.D., is an Assistant Professor of English at the University at Albany, SUNY, where she teaches courses in Women's Writing and African American and Feminist Rhetoric. She is the author of *Rhetorical Healing: The Reeducation of Contemporary Black Womanhood* and *Getting to Know Him: Observations and Experiences from My Walk of Faith*.

HARVEY CHARLES

Harvey Charles serves as Dean for International Education and Vice Provost for Global Strategy at the University at Albany, SUNY. He has been in the field of international education for more than 25 years, serving as Chief International Officer at a number of institutions around the United States. His leadership at one institution led to winning the prestigious Paul Simon Award for Comprehensive Internationalization. He has also served as president of the Association of International Education Administrators, the leading association worldwide for university leaders of international higher education. In addition to being a long-serving university administrator, Charles has published on issues including global learning, internationalizing the curriculum, and comprehensive internationalization.

DANNÉ E. DAVIS

Danné E. Davis is Associate Professor of Elementary Education at Montclair State University in New Jersey. She has published and presented papers about diversity in teacher education. Dr. Davis is currently examining LGBT children's picture storybooks as teacher education tools. She is the recipient of several awards.

PATRINA DUHANEY

Patrina Duhaney is currently pursuing her Ph.D. in Social Work. Her doctoral research examines heterosexual Black women's experiences of being charged and/or arrested by the police with an offence within the context of intimate partner abuse (IPA). Her other research interests include anti-oppression, Black feminism, critical race, intersectionality, critical race feminism, antiracist, and anticolonial studies. Patrina is also employed as a field facilitator. Among her responsibilities, she teaches the integrative seminar course and supervises graduate students completing their field placements.

TERESA GILLIAMS

Teresa Gilliams, Fulbright Scholar (Greece) 2011–2012, is Chair and Associate Professor of English at Albright College in Reading, Pennsylvania, where she teaches a wide variety of courses, including The Harlem Renaissance, Black Women Writers, and Hip-Hop. She is also the faculty adviser to Xion Step Team and African American Society, student organizations at Albright. Her research and teaching focus broadly on the representations of black women's bodies in 19th- and 20th-century, African American texts. Forthcoming is the publication of her first book titled *The Fiction of Gayl Jones: Revisioning the Black Female Body*. She is currently working on a second book project titled *Retrievable Wrongs: Reading and Preserving Black Women's Writing, 1950–2015,* which addresses the ongoing need to continue the work of recovering and providing access to important texts by black women writers.

AMEENA GHAFFAR-KUCHER

Ameena Ghaffar-Kucher, Ed.D., is a Senior Lecturer and Associate Director of the International Educational Development Program at the University of Pennsylvania's Graduate School of Education. She earned her doctorate in International Educational Development with a specialization in Curriculum and Teaching from Teachers College, Columbia University. Her research interests lie in the areas of migration and education, curriculum and pedagogy, and issues pertaining to school climate. She is coeditor (with Lesley Bartlett) of the volume *Refugees, Immigrants, and Education in the Global South: Lives in Motion*. She is also an advisory board member for MTV's "Look Different" campaign, which aims to give youth tools to be able to discuss and respond to (hidden) biases in society.

PAMELA HARRIS

Dr. Pamela E. Harris is a Mexican American Assistant Professor of Mathematics at Williams College. She received her Ph.D. from the University of Wisconsin at Milwaukee in May 2012. Her research interests focus on combinatorial problems related to representation theory. Dr. Harris established and organized the Women of Color in the Mathematical Sciences Speaker Series at USMA in 2012–2013, 2014–2015, and Minorities in Mathematics Speaker Series in 2015–2016. Dr. Harris co-organizes multiple Scientific Symposia at the SACNAS (Society for Advancement of Chicanos/Hispanics and Native Americans in Science) National Conference every year and in 2015 was one of the instructors for a short course at the Modern Math Workshop. Dr. Harris, in collaboration with Dr. Prieto Langarica, co-organized a Scientific Symposia during the 2014 SACNAS national conference titled "Young Latinas in Math and Computer Science."

DAVID MANUEL HERNÁNDEZ

David Hernández is Assistant Professor of Latina/o Studies at Mount Holyoke College. His research focuses on immigration enforcement—in particular, the U.S. detention regime. He is completing a book manuscript on this institution titled *Undue Process: Immigrant Detention and Lesser Citizenship* and he is also the coeditor of *Critical Ethnic Studies: A Reader* (2016). His work has appeared in journals such as *Border-Lines*, *Harvard Journal of Hispanic Policy*, *Journal of Race and Policy*, *Latina/o Studies*, and *NACLA: Report on the Americas*.

ANDREA G. HUNTER

Dr. Andrea G. Hunter is an Associate Professor in the Department of Human Development and Family Studies and the Director of the School of Health and Human Sciences Office of Diversity and Inclusion at The University of North Carolina at Greensboro. She is engaged in the interdisciplinary study of African American families and well-being; and her scholarship tackles interrelated questions that are central to debates about the functioning of black families. Underlying this work is an emphasis on the influences of race, gender, social class, culture, and social history on family life, the life course, and well-being. As a public intellectual, Dr. Hunter has also explored themes related to race, culture, and politics; and identity, history, and memory, with an emphasis on social justice and what connects us as a human community.

UZMA JAMIL

Dr. Uzma Jamil's research is in critical Muslim studies, focusing on how power works in the relationship between Muslim minorities and white majorities in the West. She has previously published on racialized Muslim minorities in Quebec and the securitization of Muslims in the global war on terror. Among her research areas is analysis of the linkages between Islamophobia, Orientalism, and institutional whiteness. Dr. Jamil is a member of the editorial board of *ReOrient: The Journal of Critical Muslim Studies*.

LANI V. JONES

Lani V. Jones, Ph.D., L.C.S.W., is an Associate Professor at the University at Albany, School of Social Welfare. Dr. Jones holds a doctorate and masters degree from Boston College, Boston, Massachusetts, and a B.A. from the University of Washington, Seattle, Washington. Dr. Jones's research and scholarship interests are concentrated in the area of black feminism, mental health, and evidenced-based practice with a focus on psychosocial competence enhancement. More specifically, her research has focused on the use of group work in enhancing psychosocial competence among black women. She is the author and coauthor of the book *African Americans and Depression*, several articles, and book chapters. She is also leading two research projects on health and mental health outcomes among black women, toward the development of culturally congruent services. Dr. Jones is a nationally recognized speaker on mental health practice interventions with traditionally underserved populations and has served on numerous national, state, and local health, human, and social service boards toward the advancement of social justice for black women and their families.

SONJA LANEHART

Sonja L. Lanehart, Professor and Brackenridge Endowed Chair in Literature and the Humanities at the University of Texas at San Antonio, received her B.A. from the University of Texas at Austin and her M.A. and Ph.D. from the University of Michigan. She is a former Ford Foundation Post-Doctoral Fellow, Ford Foundation Pre-Doctoral Fellow awardee, Andrew W. Mellon Fellow, Lilly Teaching Fellow, and a member of Phi Beta Kappa National Honor Society and Phi Kappa Phi National Honor Society. Dr. Lanehart has won grants from the National Science Foundation and other agencies. She has taught at the University of Georgia and the University of Texas at San Antonio. Her teaching and research interests include sociolinguistics; language, literacy, and education in African American communities; language and identity; African American women's language; motivation, self-efficacy, and resilience; goals and possible selves; and language variation and education. Dr. Lanehart has published on all of the above interests. She is the author of *Sista, Speak! Black Women Kinfolk Talk about Language and Literacy* (2002), which received Honorable Mention in the 2003 Myers Outstanding Book Award competition sponsored by the Gustavus Myers Center for the Study of Bigotry and Human Rights in North America, editor of *Sociocultural and Historical Contexts of African American English* (2001), and *African American Women's Language: Discourse, Education, and Identity* (2009). She recently published *The Oxford Handbook of African American Language* (2015).

ALICIA PRIETO LANGARICA

Dr. Alicia Prieto Langarica is a Mexican Assistant Professor at Youngstown State University. She received her Ph.D. from the University of Texas at Arlington in August 2012. Her research interests focus on applications of mathematics to biology and the social sciences, especially in upscaling discrete individual-based models to population level continuous models. Dr. Prieto Langarica established and organized a speaker series for National Hispanic Heritage Month at YSU that brought speakers yearly to YSU in 2013–2015. Just recently Dr. Prieto Langarica, in collaboration with Dr. Harris, were awarded Center for Undergraduate Research in Mathematics grants that support six undergraduate students (three at Williams and three at YSU) to work on research projects in representation theory of Lie algebras.

KHADIJAH MILLER

Khadijah Miller is an associate professor of Interdisciplinary Studies and chair of the Department of History and Interdisciplinary Studies at Norfolk State University. Her areas of specialty and publications include U.S. Black Women's history (20th century), interdisciplinarity, and online learning. Along with her chairing responsibilities, she enjoys teaching classes on The Black Woman and Interdisciplinary Studies and developing programming that focuses on the complexities of African American life, culture, and experience. She is the happy mother of two.

DELORES MULLINGS

Delores V. Mullings, B.A., B.S.W., M.S.W., Ph.D., is an Associate Professor at Memorial University of Newfoundland in the School of Social Work. Her scholarly interests are aligned with the concept of antiblack racism and the theoretical orientation of Critical Race Theory through which she explores topics such as black mothering, health and social needs of older black Caribbean Canadian adults and black queer older adults. Her other areas of interest include service learning, the scholarship of teaching and learning, institutional racism, and newcomers in rural and small urban centers.

VIVIAN NG

Vivian Ng is Chair of the Department of Women's, Gender, and Sexuality Studies at the University at Albany, State University of New York. She is a documentary filmmaker, short story writer, and historian. She has been teaching full-time at the university level since 1982. She can be reached at vng@albany.edu.

MATTHEW OWARE

Matthew Oware is the outgoing Chair of the Sociology and Anthropology department at DePauw University. He served two terms from 2010 to 2016. Moreover, he was the first person of color to serve as chair of his department. His research examines the intersections of race, culture, and masculinity with multiple publications in peer-reviewed journals.

MARY PATTILLO

Mary Pattillo is the Harold Washington Professor of Sociology and African American Studies at Northwestern University. Her areas of research and teaching include race and inequality, housing, urban politics, education reform, and stratification within the Black community. She is the author of the award-winning book *Black Picket Fences: Privilege and Peril among the Black Middle Class*, along with dozens of other scholarly and popular publications.

CHAVELLA PITTMAN

Chavella T. Pittman, Ph.D., Associate Professor of sociology at Dominican University, has research interests that include interpersonal oppression (e.g., race, gender, sexual orientation) and higher education. She is also a faculty development coach who nurtures effective faculty with strategies for efficient course planning, contextualized teaching evaluations, inclusive college classrooms and institutional assessment and change. She can be reached at http://www.effectivefaculty.org/ or chavella@effectivefaculty.org. Her publications include *Multicultural Education and Social Justice Actions* (2009), *Race and Gender Oppression in the Classroom: The Experiences of Women Faculty of Color with White Male Students* (2010), and "Exploring How African American Faculty Cope with Classroom Racial Stressors" (*The Journal of Negro Education*, 2010).

JOSE SANTOS

Jose Leonardo Santos received his B.A. in Anthropology from Brown University in 1999 and his Ph.D. in Cultural Anthropology from Southern Methodist University in 2008. His first field research occurred in Guatemala, under the NGO CADECO, as he explored the healing techniques of Chuj Maya in 1999 and 2000. In graduate school, he researched immigrant incorporation among Hispanics in North Texas. His dissertation, published as "Evangelicalism and Masculinity," focused on the influence of Evangelical Christianity on masculinity in El Salvador. Since 2011, he has focused on teaching and diversity initiatives at Metropolitan State University in Saint Paul, Minnesota. Following summer field explorations in New Mexico in 2016, he is writing on the relationship between masculinity, public discourse, and the work to end domestic violence.

JENNIFER SIMS

Jennifer Patrice Sims earned a Ph.D. from the University of Wisconsin-Madison and is a sociologist whose research specializes in race/ethnicity, social psychology and gender and sexuality. She has published both academic and popular press articles examining racial perception and mixed race identity, as well as edited the book *The Sociology of Harry Potter*. As an Adjunct Professor of Sociology at the University of Wisconsin-River Falls, she teaches a variety of courses including Introduction to Sociology, Social Psychology, Human Sexuality, Sociology of Diversity, and Research Methods.

JEFFRIANNE WILDER

Dr. JeffriAnne Wilder is a sociologist and scholar specializing in diversity, race relations, and gender issues. She is currently a tenured Associate Professor of Sociology and the Founding Director of the Institute for the Study of Race and Ethnic Relations at the University of North Florida. She holds a Ph.D. in Sociology from the University of Florida. In addition to her studies in sociology, Dr. Wilder also completed a concentration in Women's Studies and Gender Research. She completed her M.A. in Sociology from Cleveland State University and a B.A. from Allegheny College. Her areas of research interest include race and ethnic relations, minorities in higher education, women of color in the United States, qualitative methodology, and the sociology of teaching and learning.

ALFORD YOUNG JR.

Alford A. Young Jr. is Arthur F. Thurnau Professor and Chair of the Department of Sociology at the University of Michigan. He also holds an appointment in the Department of Afroamerican and African Studies. He received his M.A. and Ph.D. in Sociology from the University of Chicago, and his B.A. in Sociology, Psychology, and African American Studies from Wesleyan University. Professor Young has pursued research on low-income, urban-based African Americans; African American scholars and intellectuals; and the classroom-based experiences of faculty as they pertain to diversity and multiculturalism. He has published *The Minds of Marginalized Black Men: Making Sense of Mobility, Opportunity, and Future Life Chances* (2004), coauthored *The Souls of WEB Du Bois* (2006), and coedited *Faculty Identities and the Challenges of Diversity: Reflections on Teaching in Higher Education*. He is Chair of the Board of Directors for the YMCA of Ann

Arbor (Michigan) and serves on the Board of Trustees of Wesleyan University.

CPSIA information can be obtained
at www.ICGtesting.com
Printed in the USA
BVOW03s0016310117
474875BV00001B/1/P